GREENLAND

Disko

Godhavn

Godthaab

Sydproven

C. Farewell

DENMARK STRAIT

ICELAND

REYKJAVIK

70°

60°

50°

40°

30°

20°

Le Hbr.

Battle Hbr.
Belle Isle

Till Cove

C. Bonavista
Hearts Content
St. Johns

St. Pierre

ROES WELCOME SOUND

Whale Pt.

Daly Bay

Bailey Is.

CHESTERFIELD INLET

Wad I.
Promise I.
Fairway I.

Depot I.
Whalers

Mr. Johnson
Eskimo Camp
Baker Foreland

Marble Is.

Majestic Storehouse

Fose

N.E. ULTRA STRAIT

C. Handell

Bay of God's Mercy

Variation
S annum

92° 91° 90° 89° 88° 87° 86°

64°

63°

62°

91° 90° 89° 88° 87° 86°

AZORES
(Port)

Flores

Graciosa
Fayal   Terceira
Picos San Jorge
S. Miguel

40°

GW00722349

MERCHANT SEAMEN

BOOKS IN THE

SEAFARING MEN: THEIR SHIPS AND TIMES SERIES

SERIES EDITOR: ROBERT WOLK, Head, Library Services
Seamens Church Institute of New York
and New Jersey

MERCHANT SEAMEN

A Short History of Their Struggles

by William L. Standard

EARL M. COLEMAN, Publisher

Stanfordville, New York   1979

Library of Congress Cataloging in Publication Data

Standard, William L.
　　Merchant seamen.

　　(Seafaring men, their ships and times series)
　　Reprint of the 1947 ed. published by
International Publishers, New York.
　　Bibliography: p.
　　Includes index.
　　1. Trade-unions—Merchant seamen—United
States—History.　I. Title.　II. Series.
HD6515.S4S7　1979　　331.88′11′38750973　　79-22679
ISBN 0-930576-30-6

This Earl M. Coleman edition of MERCHANT SEAMEN is a faithful facsimile
reproduction of the first edition published in New York in 1947. This edition
reprinted by arrangement with International Publishers Co., Inc.

© 1979 by Earl M. Coleman Enterprises, Inc., Conklin Hill Road, Stanfordville,
New York 12581

Manufactured in the United States of America

MERCHANT SEAMEN

Merchant Seamen

A Short History of Their Struggles

WILLIAM L. STANDARD

INTERNATIONAL PUBLISHERS, NEW YORK

CONTENTS

5

8 CONTENTS

TO STELLA AND MICHAEL

PREFACE

This book was written during the past two years in the time that could be spared from a reasonably busy professional life. The influx of a vast number of young seamen into the merchant marine during the war made apparent the need of acquainting the workers in the industry with the struggles that preceded the formation of the present maritime unions.

Although during World War I the organization of merchant seamen in trade unions was rapid, it was also shortlived. By 1922, as a result of a series of strikes, almost all maritime unions were destroyed, and until 1934, for all practical purposes, were dead.

Since 1934 and up to the present time, while the workers in such basic industries as coal and railroad transportation had a long history of development, maritime workers' struggles to organize trade unions in their industry are of comparatively recent origin. Their growth and development during a little more than a decade brought forth every known strategem on the part of the shipowners to keep them from growing and retaining their organizational strength.

The story told here is the experience typical of all American labor except that maritime workers were forced to withstand the attacks directed against them during a

11

comparatively short period of time. During the coming decade the struggles will be intensified and will, undoubtedly, be more trying than the preceding ones. It is my hope that the account that follows will be helpful.

The maritime workers must learn thoroughly the story of past struggles and profit from the experiences in these struggles.

I wish to acknowledge my deep appreciation to Ray Torr who read the last draft of the manuscript and gave most helpful assistance.

Chapter One

IN THE BEGINNING

One-fourth of those who signed the Declaration of Independence were engaged in commerce, navigation, or contraband. Most New England merchants were smugglers. Many of the members of the Continental Congress were ship merchants or inherited their fortunes from rich shippers. Robert Morris and John Hancock were among them.

As early as 1758 the powerful shipping merchants in the City of New York combined to lower the wage scale of ship carpenters, able seamen and laborers and six years later there was set up in the same city what was, perhaps, the first colony-wide employers association. Each member of this association agreed not to "receive in his service" any workers who could not produce "a Recommendation in writing from the Master or Mistress whom he last served in this Colony." Thus, the "open shop" and "blacklisting" antedate even the Revolutionary War.

It is also interesting to note that as early as 1765, the revolutionary bodies which were established to fight England, such as the "Sons of Liberty," were in the main composed of laborers, carpenters, shipwrights, caulkers, seamen and masons. In 1770 the coopers in New York City had determined "not to sell casks except in accordance with the rates established." For this action, the coopers were tried and convicted of a conspiracy to restrain trade, and were ordered to pay 50 shillings to "the church or pious uses." The coopers who worked for the City were dismissed. While the coopers were charged with a conspiracy in restraint of trade, no such action appears to have been brought against the employers association which was a combination of employers discriminating against workers.

The Constitutional Convention of 1787 had many shippers' spokesmen among the delegates. Before the Revolution and for several decades thereafter, they were the pillars of society and played an important part in law making.

The first Congress, after the adoption of the Constitution, provided for arrest and imprisonment of seamen for desertion. The early penalty of branding on the cheek with an anchor was abandoned for the more enlightened penalty of imprisonment.

In 1792, the Criminal Code defined disobedience to an order of a superior, even within the Admiralty Waters of the United States, as mutiny. (As recently as 1943 the United States Supreme Court reaffirmed that to be the law today. Its effect on collective bargaining can be imagined.)

During the Napoleonic Wars the growth of our Merchant Marine was somewhat retarded. Both England and France interfered with our shipping. To maintain peace, President Jefferson was compelled to impose embargoes. Seamen as well as shippers suffered.

Militant struggles to alleviate conditions of workers in the early days found sailors in the vanguard. A sailor's strike took place in New York as early as March, 1800. It resulted in an open clash with the authorities, which was reported in a Baltimore newspaper on April 11, 1800, as follows:

A large mob of sailors who had turned out for higher wages, and were parading the streets in Fell's Pt., on Monday, in riotous confusion, made an attempt after dark to board and rifle a vessel belonging to Messrs. David Steward and Sons, on board of which it was said, men had entered at $18 per month. Their design being learnt, several citizens put themselves on board, to defend her in case of necessity, from the ravages of the mob, who seemed bent on mischief, and approached with drums and fife, and colors flying. As they attempted to get on board they were opposed, when a severe conflict ensued, and notwithstanding the vessel lay close alongside the wharf, they were three times repulsed, with broken heads and bloody noses. Mr. David Steward, Mr. J. Beeman, and several others who were on board, we learn, were very considerably wounded—but fortunately no lives were lost.

Philip S. Foner, in his authoritative book entitled *History of the Labor Movement in the United States,* discusses the significance of this particular demonstration of strength. It seems that the seamen had struck for a wage increase and scabs were put on board to work the ship. The march of the seamen was a manifestation of hatred for the scabs. The infuriated seamen engaged in this bloody battle with the gang who were at the ship to protect the rats. Scabbing during a strike, even as far back as 1800, was considered the vilest offense a worker could commit.

In a court in Philadelphia during a labor trial in the year 1806 a cordwainer was fined $5 for contempt of court for shouting "a scab is a shelter for lice."

Another strike of New York seamen occurred in 1802. They demanded $14 a month instead of the $10 they had been receiving. This struggle was promptly smashed by the militia.

The British Navy, during the Napoleonic Wars, was contemptuous of our sovereign rights, pirated our commerce, and impressed our seamen into its service. The War of 1812, however, checked the arrogance of the English. A healthy respect for the valor of the American seamen was instilled.

The character of the Yankee sailor was described in the following glowing terms by an English Parliamentary Committee:

He was a consummate master of his calling, a keen lookout, a clever helmsman, bold and active aloft, of iron-like physique, famed the world round for his vigor and endurance.

AMERICAN SHIPPING PROSPERS

After the War of 1812, American shipping began to prosper and, with the exception of a short period following the 1837 depression, continued to do so until the Civil War.

During this period, the change from sailing vessels to steam and from wooden ships to iron and steel was taking place. But we clung to the wooden sailing vessels for some time. This was partly because our shipyards were geared to the building of wooden ships, partly because our iron and steel industry was not as far advanced as that of the English, and partly because of the challenge to American skill and resourcefulness.

England, however, not only made the change early in the century but recognized that the maintenance of a strong merchant marine was a responsibility of the government. The British began to subsidize the building of the new iron steamships.

As early as 1838, Samuel Cunard and his associates received an Atlantic mail subsidy of $425,000 from the English government. England was bent on meeting American competition by subsidizing British companies.

In 1847, the United States government granted a subsidy to the Collins Line and five years later granted one to the Pacific Mail Line. As soon as government aid was given to our shippers, they began to recapture trade. In 1852 the Collins Line carried 4,306 passengers while Cunard carried only 2,969.

Opposition to subsidies arose in the decade before the Civil War. Although the Crimean War of 1856, because of the demand for ships, was a shot in the arm for the American shippers, the Civil War brought that demand to an end.

The British during this period not only subsidized shipping and shipbuilding, but attacked the American industry by imposing all kinds of unwarranted demands on American shipowners who were seeking marine insurance in Great Britain. For example, they required all American built ships to be "refastened" in England before they could apply for marine insurance.

ECONOMIC RIVALRIES

The full extent and nature of the "economic rivalry between Great Britain and the United States" is clearly illustrated in a book under that name by Professor J. Fred Rippy. On page 109, he wrote:

If hostile nations must fight, the United States would furnish them with supplies, building up its trade and shipping at their expense . . . England, on the contrary, viewed commercial questions from the angle of a great belligerent sea power whose security and prosperity depend almost entirely upon the domination of the ocean.

Lord Liverpool, British Prime Minister from 1812 to 1827, stated this issue very clearly in 1824. To him the most "formidable" phase of the Spanish-American question was this very matter of sea power. "The great and favorite object of the policy of Britain, for more than four centuries," he said, "has been to foster and encourage our navigation, as the basis of our maritime power. In this branch of national industry the people of the United States have become more formidable rivals to us than any nation which has ever existed . . . The views and policy of the North Americans seems mainly directed toward supplanting us in navigation in every quarter of the globe, but more particularly in the seas contiguous to America.

"Let us recollect that as their commercial marine is augmented, their military marine must proportionately increase. And it cannot be doubted that, if we provoke the new states of America (South American Republics) to give a decided preference in their ports to the people of the United States over ourselves, the navigation of these expansive dominions will be lost to us, and it will in a great measure, be transferred to our rivals . . .

"I am conscientiously convinced that if we allow these new states to consolidate their system and policy with the United States of America, it will in a very few years prove fatal to our greatness, if not endanger our safety."

The political and economic issues so sharply outlined by Lord Liverpool in 1824 can be very well taken to heart by proponents of this Good Neighbor policy. Economic rivalries in South America and elsewhere have not been removed.

Chapter Two

AMERICAN SHIPPING DECLINES

Cornelius Vanderbilt, founder of one of America's big fortunes, helped retard the establishment of a sound American merchant marine. A Senate investigating committee in 1858 revealed how Vanderbilt, by the threat of establishing competing lines or of submitting a competing bid, extorted bribes from those who were granted subsidies.

Out of one mail subsidy grant by Congress of $900,000 a year, Vanderbilt compelled payment to himself of $56,000 a month or $672,000.

The Civil War ended the development of the American Merchant Marine. That there no longer was any profit in shipping is conclusively established by the fact that Commodore Cornelius Vanderbilt left this field and began his career as a railroad owner.

Gustavus Myers, author of *History of the Great American Fortunes,* has the following to say regarding the origin of the Vanderbilt fortune:

A very large portion of this came directly from his bold system of commercial blackmail. The mail subsidies were the real foundation of his fortune. Many newspaper editorials and articles of the time mention this fact. Only a few of the important underlying facts of the character of his methods when he was in the steamboat and steamship business can be gleaned from the records. But these few give a clear enough insight. With a part of the proceeds of his plan of piracy, he carried on a subtle system of corruption by which he and the other steamer owners were able time after time not only to continue their control of Congress and the postal authorities, but to defeat postal reform measures.

The post Civil War period saw a change in the interest of our industrialists. Tremendous profits were to be made in the building of railroads and the development of the west. Revolutions in Europe had resulted in millions of immigrants. From Germany alone more than 2,000,000 migrated to this country after the defeat of the Revolution of 1848.

The drive inland resulted in a complete loss of interest in shipping. The preoccupation of Congress with the development of the interior and the neglect of shipping almost resulted in the complete elimination of the American merchant vessels.

By 1880 American ships carried no more than 13 per cent of our imports and exports. By 1900 only 7.1 per cent of American shipping was carried in American ships. We had, in 1900, but 826,694 tons of American shipping sailing the seas.

After the Civil War, one feeble attempt was made to give aid to American shipping. That was in 1867 when the Pacific Mail Company was granted a subsidy of $500,000 a year to carry mail to the Orient.

Only one new American shipping company was organized in 1872. The American Steamship Company of Philadelphia built four iron steamers for the North Atlantic trade. This company was able to operate without a subsidy only because the powerful Pennsylvania Railroad Company guaranteed cargoes.

During the same period, the White Star and Cunard Lines were subsidized by the British government and even an American Line, the Inman Line, received a British subsidy to carry mail.

In 1901 the Inman Line was the only American Line carrying British mail. In addition to its British subsidy it was also receiving an annual subsidy of $528,537 from the United States. The Cunard Line was receiving a subsidy of $213,103. In addition, the United States paid $91,591 for mail service to the White Star (British) steamers; $80,141 to North German Lloyd steamers; $52,750 to the Hamburg American (German) steamers; $24,842 to the General Transatlantic (French) steamers. Thus foreign lines were receiving as much as domestic lines.

LOT OF THE SEAMEN

While our government was liberally subsidizing foreign shipowners, however, the seamen on our own ships were exposed to most inhuman working conditions. Brutal practices of ships' officers, carryovers from the notorious slave trade days, continued. American ships, because of these conditions, were sometimes referred to as "hell ships." The conduct of these officers created such a scandal that in 1871 Congress passed a statute authorizing the lifting of officers' certificates for such misconduct.

Because it was so difficult to obtain seamen during this period, the practice of shanghaiing was resorted to. The practice of obtaining blood money also grew up. Blood money was a fee obtained by a shipping crimp for supplying drugged and intoxicated sailors on board a ship.

The shipping crimps were boarding house keepers who controlled the labor market. Sailors were given advances in the form of board, lodging, and liquor. The crimp could keep the sailor's clothing for his debt. The Shipmaster would then advance to the crimp the amount of the sailor's debt and secure the services of the seaman. This evil, after a while, began to be felt by the shipowners as well as the seamen, as they were forced to pay bribes to the ship-master in order to get crews. The shipping crimps extorted money from the seaman for the job he was furnished, and from the ship owner, for the crew he provided.

To put an end to these abuses, Congress passed the Shipping Commissioner's Act of 1872. Under it, masters were required to bring prospective crews before a shipping commissioner. Articles had to be signed in his presence. This put an end to shanghaiing.

The master was also required on his return to the first continental port to present the articles and his crew to a shipping commissioner. This was to prevent abandonment of seamen in foreign ports.

But while this act protected the sailor against the brutal practices then prevalent, it also provided that he be imprisoned for desertion. The real effect of this law was to guarantee the shipowner with a crew.

In 1874 the Shipping Commissioner's Act of 1872 was amended to exempt seamen employed on vessels in coastwise and Great Lakes trade from the provision of that law which made desertion punishable by imprisonment. The effect of this exemption for Great Lakes and coastwise seamen on organization of maritime unions will be seen presently.

Chapter Three

LAKES SEAMEN ORGANIZE

The first permanent union of merchant seamen in the United States, the Lakes Seamen's Union, was organized in 1878, although maritime unions are known to have existed in the Lakes area as far back as 1863.

During the Civil War there existed in the Rivers and Lakes a very strong pilots' union. This group of workers was undoubtedly the highest paid craft in the country at that time. Their strong union in no small measure was responsible for their high wages.

Before the railroads were able to carry any appreciable quantity of the freight from the midwest to the Atlantic Coast, Great Lakes shipping was the most convenient and most economical means of transportation. Agricultural products, during seasons, moved east and industrial products moved west on Lakes boats. The short sailing season and the concentration of seamen in the large cities made possible early organization of Lakes boatmen.

To check any progress of unionization on the Great Lakes, the Lake Carriers Association was formed in 1885. Since its founding this association has constantly sought to impose an anti-union policy on the Great Lakes.

In 1895 the International Seamen's Union was founded and the Lakes Seamen's Union became affiliated to it. At the 1900 convention, Great Lakes delegates represented 3,587 members as against 2,072 for the Pacific Coast, and 1,150 for the Atlantic Coast.

The Spanish-American War increased the demand for steel, and shipping on the Lakes boomed. The militancy of the Great Lakes seamen mounted, resulting in the consummation of agreements with the shipowners in that area, which, for the first time, established hiring through the union hall.

HIGH WATERMARK

The decade preceding the panic of 1907 may be considered the high watermark of collective bargaining on the Lakes and, for that matter, anywhere in the maritime industry up to that time.

For five years, from 1903 to 1908, the Lake Carriers Association was required to hire all unlicensed personnel from the Lakes Seamen's Union. At first, the union was required to supply men within twenty-four hours. Since at times this was impossible, the time was changed in subsequent agreements to seventy-two hours.

This progress was, however, short-lived. In 1901, various steel companies on the Lakes were merged into the newly organized United States Steel Corp. The Pittsburgh Steamship Company, a U. S. Steel subsidiary, operating in the Lakes, began to assume a dominant role in Lakes shipping.

In 1908, taking advantage of the business slump, the Lake Carriers Association declared open warfare on the seamen's unions. At a special meeting of the association the following resolutions were adopted:

1. That the owners of ships on the Great Lakes do now declare that the open shop principle be adopted and adhered to on all ships.

2. That the Lake Carriers Association stands for the foregoing principle.

3. That the matter be referred to the executive committee with full power to act and carry out this principle.

WELFARE PLAN

The Association also inaugurated its notorious "welfare plan" in 1908, to keep "troublemakers," "agitators," and "malcontents" off their ships. Its essential features were:

1. "Assembly rooms" where "welfare certiècates" and $1 per year dues were required for employment.
2. "Continuous Discharge Book" with entries of "good" or "fair" conduct for guidance of officers.
3. Death benefit and savings plan which competed with the union for the seaman's loyalty.

Other means of attacking the unions included (1) the recruiting of a large surplus of job applicants, especially of young men and boys who had never worked on the Lakes; (2) giving special privileges to unlicensed officers and encouraging them to seek out and discharge all union men; (3) paying higher wages than previous union agreements provided for; and (4) maintenance of an espionage system.

For a full year after the attack on the Lakes Seamen's Union was begun, efforts were made to compromise without success. On May 1, 1909, the weakened union called a strike. It continued for a year and resulted in a smashing of the union.

STRIKE THREATENED DURING WORLD WAR I

The anti-labor policy of the association expressed itself in its most ugly form during World War I.

In September, 1917, the Lakes unlicensed seamen,

who had rebuilt their union, announced their intention of striking on October 1. Government investigators were sent down to inquire into the "Welfare Plan," which, the seamen said, was used to hamper organization. Before strike action could be taken, the Lakes froze and the season ended. In the spring of 1918, a strike was again threatened. The only concession that the Lake Carriers Association would make was the substitution of a "Certificate of Membership" for the Continuous Discharge Book. But the certificate had attached to it a pocket where all discharge papers had to be deposited.

Finally the United States Shipping Board directed that employment could be obtained without presentation of either book or discharge certificate. The strike was thus averted.

The war was no sooner over than the Lake Carriers Association renewed its anti-labor policy. In 1921 it reintroduced the Continuous Discharge Book and cut wages 25 per cent. At a conference in Washington, the Association renewed the open shop policy that it had adopted in 1908.

The Lakes seamen struck the following year, but the strike was immediately smashed.

Chapter Four

EAST AND WEST COASTS ORGANIZE

Seamen on the West Coast were not long in following the example of their brothers on the Lakes. The Coast Seamen's Union was formed in 1885, largely through the efforts of one Sigismund Danielwicz, a member of the International Workingmen's Association. It came about this way:

In the spring of 1885, Danielwicz urged seamen in San Francisco to form a protective union and join hands with all other labor organizations in that city. Danielwicz, Burnette G. Haskell, and Martin M. Schneider, all members of the International Workingmen's Association, together with organizers representing the Knights of Labor, addressed an assemblage and took steps to organize the seamen. Few of them at that time had money to pay the entrance fee and although more than two hundred signed petitions to organize the union, hardly enough money was collected to pay for the hiring of the hall. It was under such auspices that the organization of seamen first began.

About its organization Professor Paul S. Taylor, in his *Sailors Union of the Pacific*, has this to say:

The International Workingmen's Association, founded by Karl Marx, was represented in San Francisco by a group of enthusiasts whose ambition was to organize as many trades

27

as possible. Perhaps chief among these was Burnette G. Haskell, a young lawyer of magnetic personality and a persuasive speaker. Not a laboring man by birth or training, he had nevertheless become an ardent worker for the betterment of the working classes.

It was he who with a few other organizers from the International had played such a prominent part in aiding and stimulating the organization of the Coast Seamen's Union and had fired the zeal of the cooks and waiters with his oratory. So when in May the steamshipmen gathered in little groups along the wharves to discuss the demand for better hours, and an organization to enforce it, Haskell again appeared on the waterfront to fire the enthusiasm of the sailors to organize for their own protection and uplift. An informal meeting was held on the Broadway dock, and it was decided to form a union.

In 1891 the Coast Seamen's Union was amalgamated with an organization known as the Steamship Sailors Union. They adopted the name, Sailors' Union of the Pacific. In 1888 the first permanent organization of seamen on the Atlantic Coast was begun. None of these unions, however, was able to do much about wages and local conditions.

NATIONAL SEAMEN'S UNION

It was not until 1892 when the National Seamen's Union was organized under the auspices of the American Federation of Labor that a foundation for effective organizational work of seamen was laid. At the 1895 National Seamen's Union (NSU) convention, the name was changed to International Seamen's Union of America.

When the International Seamen's Union constitution was finally worked out at the beginning of the century, it was a federation of affiliated autonomous unions, similar in structure and function to the AFL with which it was affiliated. By the time the 1921 strike took place it had nineteen different craft unions and sectional unions.

Charters were handed out to small groups in cities. At the 1920 convention a charter was issued to the Eastern Marine Workers Association of New Haven, Connecticut. Previously a charter had been issued and reissued to the Halibut Fishermen's and Deep-Sea Fishermen's Union of the Pacific. The records do not disclose whether separate charters were issued to the salmon, sardine, mackerel, and sword-fish fishermen of each separate district but the indiscriminate chartering of craft in the various districts was bound to create jurisdictional disputes and conflicts.

Between 1909, when the Great Lakes union was smashed, and the outbreak of World War I, little progress was made by marine unions.

THE *ARAGO* CASE

Indeed, the prevailing attitude toward seamen during the first decade of this century being what it was, there is reason to wonder that they were able to organize at all. This attitude is best illustrated by a decision of the United States Supreme Court in the *Arago* case in 1897.

In May, 1895, four members of the crew of the *Arago* had jumped ship in Astoria, Oregon, where the vessel was taking on cargo for Chile. They were arrested and tried as deserters. Their defense was that their forcible return to the ship was involuntary servitude in violation of the Thirteenth Amendment.

The case was fought up to the Supreme Court where it was held that a seaman's contract of employment was exceptional because he "surrenders his personal liberty" during the life of the contract. The court declared:

Indeed, seamen are treated by Congress, as well as by the Parliament of Great Britain, as deficient in that full and intelligent responsibility for their acts which is accredited to ordinary adults, and as needing the protection of the law in the same sense in which minors and wards are entitled to the protection of their parents and guardians.

Not until 1915, after many years of struggle and with the help of Senator Robert M. LaFollette, was the shame of this decision, often referred to as the "Second Dred Scott Decision," wiped out. The Seamen's Act of 1915 not only held that seamen were no longer "slaves" but also provided for the right of seamen to demand half of wages earned and unpaid in ports of landing and discharging, and extended to foreign seamen the right to demand payment of wages on arriving in a port.

Between 1915 and 1920, the International Seamen's Union saw its largest growth. The total membership before the 1921 strike was 115,000. The Atlantic Coast district had 85,750 members as against Pacific 19,950 and the Lakes 9,300.

The craft organization set-up not only had in it the seeds of internal discord but also made the ISU vulnerable to attack from the industrial set-up of the militant Industrial Workers of the World.

As might have been expected, disputes arose constantly among the unions affiliated to the ISU. Each affiliate had a constitution of its own. The officers of each clashed at times, both sectionally and on the craft basis.

Minor differences arose between the Masters, Mates

& Pilots and the Marine Engineers Beneficial Association. The Marine Firemen's Union of the Atlantic claimed that members of the MEBA were doing some of the work usually done by the firemen. Similar differences were had with the International Association of Machinists. All these differences had their effect on the final struggle with employers which took place in 1921. The unwillingness of the longshoremen to co-operate was perhaps the fatal blow.

THE ROLE OF THE INDUSTRIAL WORKERS OF THE WORLD

International and jurisdictional disputes were stimulated by the active role played by the members of the Industrial Workers of the World. This organization based on the industrial union idea came into being as a result of dissatisfaction with the slow progress the conservative unions were making. It believed that: (a) No terms with an employer are final; all peace, so long as the wage system lasts, is but an armed truce; (b) The day of successful long strikes was passed; (c) Employers will concede only what the workers have the power to take and hold by strength of organization; therefore they sought no agreements with the employers.

In 1913, the National Industrial Union of Marine Transport Workers was formed on the East Coast. Because they were organized on an industrial basis it was natural that they should become affiliated with the IWW.

The strength of the IWW must not be minimized. According to Paul Brissenden, author of a book on the IWW, the New York branch of the Marine Transport Workers Union alone had 5,000 members.

The Marine Transport Workers Union admitted as members not only all crafts of seamen but also long-shoremen and seamen on small harbor and river craft. The officers of the various Atlantic unions of the ISU admitted that roughly 25 per cent of their membership had joined the Transport Workers Union.

IWW-ISU RIVALRY

By 1916, a new trend in IWW organizational practices was noticeable. According to Brissenden "the tenth convention is remarkable as denoting the decline in the 'Soap Boxer' as the dominant element. The dominant tone was constructive rather than controversial and the general demand was for such constitutional and other changes as would make for greater efficiency in the work of the organization." One delegate at the 1916 convention, said; "The IWW is passing out of the propaganda stage and is entering the stage of constructive organization."

In 1917 the IWW consisted of six industrial unions: (1) National Industrial Union of Marine Transport Workers, (2) The Forest and Lumber Workers Union, (3) Metal and Machinery Workers Union, (4) Iron Workers Union, (5) Railway Workers Union, and (6) Textile Workers Union. The Marine Transport Workers Union was one of its strongest affiliates.

The IWW had many weaknesses. Because it was forbidden by its constitution to enter into contracts, ISU officials felt that they would be unable to show concrete results upon the return of prosperity. Workers, they felt, would favor the organization which could show economic advantages in the form of contracts with the employer.

On the outbreak of World War I, the ISU and the

shipowners signed what they called the Atlantic War agreement. This was the first agreement ever made between the Atlantic shipowners as a body and any labor organization. This agreement was the organizational weapon which the ISU officials needed in their fight with the "radicals," as they called the IWW.

THE CALL TO THE SEA

To encourage men to join the new merchant marine, ISU President Andrew Furuseth issued his famous "Call to the Sea." It read:

The United States Government, the shipowners, the sea men jointly issue this call to the sea.

The message to those who have left the sea is this: The conditions which caused you to leave no longer exist. Seamen are no longer bound by laws to the vessels on which they serve. The seamen's act has conferred this and many other blessings upon them. Economic and working conditions affecting the calling have been immeasurably improved. Attractive wages are being paid.

This message to the young man, the novice, is this: You can give ear to the call of the sea and respond to its lure with confidence that upon the sea a career is again a possibility. The improvement in the conditions affecting the seamen's calling has necessarily increased its opportunities for the ambitious and industrious to secure advancement. Conditions on board vessels have been materially improved. When vessels are in port the seamen are as free as men ashore.

The message to all followers or would-be followers of the sea is this: The United States of America, above all other countries, has proven itself the friend of the seamen. That Nation needs you now. Our country is building many steamers and it needs the men and the officers to man them as never before.

An agreement has been reached between the shipowners and the seamen concerning conditions and wages, calculated to assure adequate recompense and reasonable comfort to those who return to the sea or for the first time respond to its lure, and such agreement has been countersigned by the Secretary of Labor, the Secretary of Commerce, and the chairman of the Shipping Board of the United States Government.

American youths answered the call. They sailed the vessels during the war as members of the ISU. They endured the hardships and faced all of the perils. The submarines took their toll then, as they did in World War II. Yet a great many began to love the calling.

With peace, however, came new problems. American seamen were now aware of the advantages of organization. In 1919 they wanted changes in working conditions, the eight-hour day in port, and three watches at sea. Most important they wanted the preferential union shop.

When the 1918 agreement was renewed, wage increases averaging $15 a month were obtained. The eight-hour day was granted with some exceptions and union delegates were granted access to the piers. This agreement was again renewed on May 1, 1920.

In January, 1921, anticipating the contract termination, the shipowners gave notice of a wage cut.

Chapter Five

THE 1921 STRIKE

Opportunities for organization had been unusually good during the war. And progress made by the ISU was duplicated in other basic industries. In 1919, the Amalgamated Association of Iron Steel and Tin Workers sought to complete organization of the steel workers. Judge Elbert H. Gary, chairman of the board, United States Steel Corp., announced that he stood for the "open shop." AFL President Samuel Gompers supported the steel organizing drive but, finally, after the steel workers were forced out on strike, broke with the strikers and attacked their leader, William Z. Foster. The strike was broken by violence, terror, and the biggest scab-herding drive in American labor history. This steel corporation campaign set the tone for the drive against labor in all industries.

Earlier, in January, 1919, the International Longshoremen's Association, the Tidewater Boatmen's Union and the Lighter Captains' Union in New York City struck for the eight-hour day. They were persuaded to return to work by the National War Labor Board. When the board's decision proved to be unsatisfactory the longshoremen struck again but were licked because the officials of the Tidewater Boatmen's Union and the Lighter Captains' Union settled and then worked with scabs.

This division in the ranks must be laid at the door of the officials of the International Seamen's Union, with which the latter unions were affiliated, a betrayal which the longshoremen remembered well in 1921.

The Judas role played by these officials was duplicated in the fatal seamen's strike of 1921.

SHIPOWNERS' OFFENSIVE

In January, 1921, the American Steamship Owners Association wrote to Percy Pryor, secretary of the Eastern and Gulf Sailors Association, proposing revision of the contract which was to terminate on May 1. The shipowners asked:

(a) Immediate elimination of overtime; (b) Readjustment of subsistence and room allowance; (c) Reduction in wages as follows: deck engineers, reduction from $100 to $75; oilers, $95 to $70; coal passers and wipers, $75 to $55 and correspondingly for other grades.

This proposed cut of a little more than 25 per cent in base wages plus elimination of overtime amounted to a reduction of from 40 to 60 per cent.

Acting chairman of the Shipping Board, Admiral Benson, co-operating with the shipowners, urged the acceptance of the shipowners' terms. Union representatives, seeking the co-operation of the Shipping Board, wrote to Admiral Benson pointing out that preservation of the American Merchant Marine required the maintenance of wage rates and working conditions. They pointed out that, whereas in 1916 only 5 per cent of the seamen working on American flag ships were native Americans, in 1921 they numbered 51 per cent.

Not only did Admiral Benson give the seamen no consideration or help, but actually co-operated with the shipowners. Andrew Furuseth wrote to President Harding asking for his consideration "in the firm faith that you will act for the development and maintenance of the merchant marine." This letter was writtten on April 29. On May 1, without waiting for an answer from the president, the shipowners locked out the seamen from their ships.

The shipowners did tender a contract containing the original conditions, plus a provision that the shipowners reserved the right to abolish the contract at any time on thirty days' notice.

The seamen immediately declared a strike.

ROLE OF THE SHIPPING BOARD

The Shipping Board co-operated with the shipowners. It declared that any shipowner who would undertake to pay the old rates would have his ships taken away from him.

Senator LaFollette, in support of a resolution to investigate the Shipping Board, stated on the floor of the Senate on July 25, 1921:

When it is remembered at the time this statement or order was issued a number of the lines were ready to sign up with men on terms more favorable than those offered by the Shipping Board, it is readily seen how this threat, which amounted to notice that allocations of ships would be withdrawn from such companies, operated to prevent a settlement.

In order to break the strike, the Shipping Board made every effort to settle with Marine Engineers Beneficial Association because it felt that the engineers' union was the backbone of the strikes.

The lengths to which the Shipping Board was willing

to go to break the strike is shown by the following quotation from Senator LaFollette's speech:

In addition to this, I have in my possession original affidavits, which if they are true, show coercion and deception on the part of the agents of the Shipping Board in procuring men to sign up for sea duty. I also have a blank form of a letter purported to be signed by a representative of the Shipping Board and used in sending non-union men, with their expenses paid, from Chicago to Seattle, to take the place of union seamen. I do not care to put these original documents into the record, but I will be glad to submit them to the committee which undertakes the investigation under the resolution I have offered.

"OPEN SHOP" DRIVE BEGINS

In June, 1921, Chairman Albert D. Lasker of the Shipping Board announced that the "open shop" would be strictly enforced in the American Merchant Marine. Admiral Benson and T. P. O'Connor, acting as a subcommittee for the board, stated plainly that the new board would not give union agents privileges of going on the docks or ships. They also stated that no new agreement would be ratified for longer than six months.

These formal statements of government officials must not be mistaken for uninspired decisions. Government officials, recognizing their responsibility for the upbuilding of the American Merchant Marine, would not have taken such action on their own—action which could only drive American seamen from American ships.

The Shipping Board, of course, was nothing more than the mouthpiece of the shipping industry—certainly at that time the most sinister influence in America. As Senator LaFollette said:

The practical operation of the Shipping Board have, to a large extent, been in the hands of a small group of shipping men, who represent in their former associations a group particularly hostile to trade unionism.

Senator LaFollette's resolution was not adopted and the Shipping Board was not investigated. The Republicans were in the saddle. They were also hungry for the pork barrel. It was not until 1935 when nearly $300,-000,000 had been appropriated and squandered and a new administration elected that an investigation was ordered.

Encouraged by the Shipping Board and completely unmolested by the servile, and, as will be later shown, corrupt officials of the ISU, the shipowners promulgated the following monthly wage rates for 1922:

Able bodied seamen	$47.50
Ordinary seamen	35.00
Boatswain	65.00
Carpenter	70.00
Fireman	50.00
Coal passer	40.00
Watertender oiler	55.00

The development of the depression in 1921 as well as the unholy alliance between the U.S. Shipping Board and the shipowners made the smashing of the strike and the union a simple matter.

Monopoly was becoming enthroned. The Harding administration and the Ohio Gang were getting underway. The denial to union representatives of the right to board the ships made it impossible for the ISU to function.

The strike called on May 1 was smashed and between 1921 and 1934, the ISU was a name only.

Before beginning the story of the struggle to bring trade unions back on board American ships, let us examine another development—a movement not only to drive unions from American ships, but actually to eliminate the American Merchant Marine from world commerce altogether.

Chapter Six

AN INTERNATIONAL CONSPIRACY

Economic rivalry between the United States and Great Britain for the South American trade ended in almost complete victory for Great Britain. That was inevitable.

All of this country's capital resources during the last quarter of the last century were employed in the development of railroads and the newly acquired territories. In spite of the growing need for a merchant fleet, nothing was done about it. At the outbreak of World War I, American tonnage had reached its lowest ebb in generations, a little over 700,000 tons.

While the United States was concentrating on the development of its own resources, England was pushing her free trade policy. She became the clearing house for world commerce. London became the banking center for international trade.

England's extensive foreign trade made necessary the

establishment of shipping agencies in major ports throughout the world.*

Our acquisition of overseas possessions following the Spanish-American War was construed by England as a threat to her shipping supremacy. With all of the American railroads pouring their industrial commodities towards the American seaports, it became apparent that unless efforts were made to frustrate the building of an American Merchant Marine, England's monopoly in shipping would be broken.

THE PLOT BEGINS

In 1901 J. P. Morgan & Co. organized the United States Steel Corporation, a merger of all the formidable steel mills in our country. The House of Morgan and Kuhn-Loeb & Co., between them, controlled 88 per cent of the American railroads.

J. P. Morgan & Co. and Morgan, Grenfell and Co. of London are closely enough related to be considered one banking house. E. C. Grenfell, a partner of Morgan, Grenfell and Co., was also a director of the Bank of England.

In 1902, soon after U. S. Steel was organized, Morgan & Co. reorganized the International Navigation Company of New Jersey and changed its name to the International Mercantile Marine. From that time on the influence of this banking house began to be felt in the shipping industry.

Within one year after the organization of the International Mercantile Marine, it entered into an agreement

*In foreign ports, ships rely on freight soliciting agencies. English freight soliciting agencies in foreign ports give preference to their bottoms as against those of other nationals.

with the British Board of Trade.   This agreement was
to run for twenty years.

The full effect of this agreement and the resulting
subservience of American shipping to British shipping
was not revealed until after World War I.

During the discussion in support of his resolutions to
investigate the Shipping Board, in July, 1921, Senator
LaFollette had the following to say with respect to the
role of British shipping interests in discouraging the establishment of an American merchant marine:

> Propaganda is the new weapon and today they [the British]
> are conducting an active campaign within our borders. Their
> object is to discourage the American people from supporting
> Congress in placing our mercantile marine upon a firm foot-
> ing ... We must be prepared to combat insidious propaganda
> calculated to nullify our efforts to secure that portion of the
> maritime commerce of the world to which we are justly
> entitled.

It is axiomatic that the successful operation of a shipping company depends, in the main, upon the guarantee
of a certain amount of cargo.   We have seen above that
the only reason why the American Steamship Company
of Philadelphia was able to operate successfully for 25
years after its organization in 1872 without the benefit of
a subsidy was because it had the support of the powerful
Pennsylvania Railroad Co.

To see how that kind of support was assured for the
newly formed International Mercantile Marine, we must
look at the board of directors of the newly organized
shipping company.

1. J.P. Morgan & Co. controlled many railroads, among
them Central Railroad of New Jersey; Lehigh Valley;
Northern Pacific; Atchison, Topeka & Santa Fe Railway;

Chicago Great Northern; and Pere Marquette.

2. The Guaranty Trust Company was represented on the board by Charles H. Sabin who held directorships in 43 different railroads.

3. The National City Bank whose president, Frank A. Vanderlip, also sat on the board of the IMM, was a director in no fewer than 31 different American railroads

UNDER BRITAIN'S HEEL

The directors of the newly organized IMM controlling the operations of almost all of the important railway lines were in the most strategic position to furnish cargoes to a newly organized American flag fleet. Such a fleet could have undermined the monopoly in shipping which England had at the beginning of the century.

The directors of the IMM, by an agreement entered into with the British board of trade, made impossible the establishment of an American flag merchant marine.

The IMM, wholly American owned, invested its capital in subsidiary shipping companies which operated ships under foreign flags. These subsidiaries owned and operated 113 vessels whose gross tonnage amounted to 1,077,728.

Out of this fleet of 113 vessels, the IMM operated directly under the American flag only 11 vessels. The balance of 102 vessels was operated by British companies under the British flag, except for two which flew the Belgian flag.

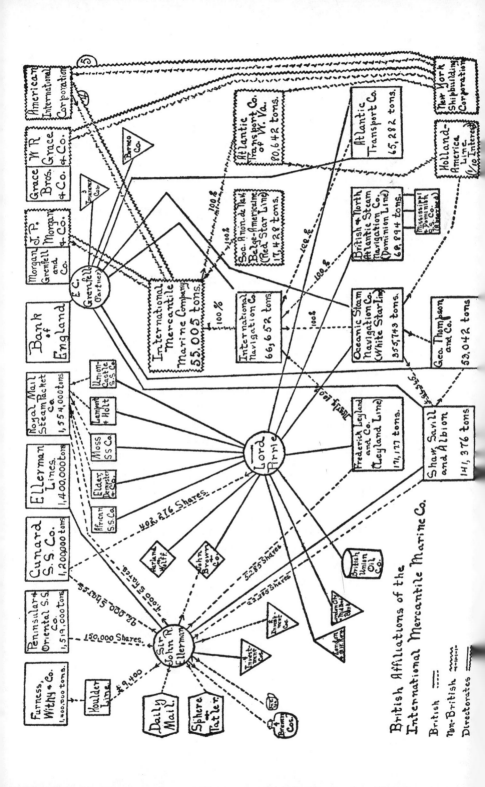

British Affiliations of the International Mercantile Marine Co.

British ———
Non-British ~~~~~~
Directorates ════

The diagram on page 44 illustrates the vast holdings of the IMM in British shipping companies. It will be noted that the IMM owned 100 per cent of the White Star, 100 percent of the Red Star Line, 100 per cent of the Dominion Line, nearly 100 per cent of the Leyland Line and a controlling and participating interest in a network of other British companies.

With respect to its British subsidiaries, the IMM bound itself to the British government by agreeing that:

1. Ships of the American owned subsidiaries were to be on an equality with all other British ships in regard to any services, such as naval, military and postal, that may be required of them.

2. A majority of the Board of Directors of those companies were to be British subjects.

3. No vessel of these subsidiaries could be sold without the consent of the British Board of Trade.

4. All of the ships' officers must be British subjects, and the nationality of the crews shall be prescribed by the British government.

5. All of the vessels operated by these subsidiaries must be sold to the British Admiralty, upon the Admiralty's demand.

6. All replacements and repairs were to be done in British yards.

7. The agreement was to run for twenty years, from September 27, 1903, and could be cancelled, on five years' notice by either side, except "that his Majesty's Government can terminate it at any time."

8. Finally, and most important, this contract was to be considered as an English contract, and all interpretations of the contract or disputes arising under it, must be re-

ferred to the Lord High Chancellor of Great Britain, whose decision, *whether on law or fact,* was to be final.

MILKING THE IMM

This agreement was reached in 1903 and amended in 1910. As early as 1910, it seems, the British Admiralty felt that war between itself and the fast growing German empire was inevitable. To further guarantee to itself use of the American-owned British-controlled International Mercantile Marine ships, the 1903 agreement was so amended in 1910 that the British Admiralty could control these ships for use as armed cruisers.

Under the 1903 agreement, British yards had to be employed to do the repair work on all foreign flag vessels of the IMM. Profits made by IMM subsidiaries were, therefore, controlled by British interests and a *net* profit upon these investments of the IMM could be made only by the grace of the British Board of Trade. So successful were these companies in milking the IMM foreign subsidiaries, that the IMM was unable to pay any dividends on its common or preferred stock, except during the World War I and a few years thereafter.

It should, therefore, be clear that in establishing the IMM and securing for it that array of railroad support, Great Britain was insured against competition from any other American shipping company that might dare to come into the field.

Respecting the British-American tie-up, Senator La-Follette had this to say in 1921:

It is quite apparent that there is a partnership here, a deal between the masters of the shipping of Great Britain and the masters of the railroads and finance of this country, and that that combination is drawing on the purse of the Government (meaning the Shipping Board) to build up what we, in our blindness, call an American Merchant Marine. . . .

You had a combination made between the great railroads of this country and British overseas shipping, and the International Mercantile Marine Co., with a sort of medium, or line, through which this organization was built. . . .

The International Mercantile Marine Co. found it more profitable to employ its capital under these contracts in conjunction with Great Britain, with her control of world commerce, than to attempt to establish an American Merchant Marine, and they made these contracts accordingly and are still operating under them.

AMERICAN SHIPS NEVER HAD A CHANCE

Senator LaFollette was convinced by his studies that the British influence in the Shipping Board was such that there was no possibility of building an American fleet. Senator Wesley L. Jones of Washington, another student of American shipping, was similarly convinced that the Shipping Board was serving the interests of British shipping and not those of American.

Senator LaFollette, on the floor of the Senate, quoted the following from a speech by Senator Jones:

A short time ago, a reputable gentleman from Newark, New Jersey, told me of his experience in attempting to establish a shipping line between Newark and England. He applied to the Shipping Board to buy or charter government ships for this purpose. His application was referred to the Shipping Board's representative in New York, and he said he was opposed to it. On being pressed for his reasons, he said that the establishment of such a line would injure business of British lines sailing out of New York.

Protection afforded to British shipping by Shipping

Board officials accounts, in part, for a story in the *Journal of Commerce* of July 14, 1921. It was reported that the appointment to the Shipping Board of William J. Love, J. Barston Smull, and A. J. Frey not only pleased American but foreign shipping interests as well.

This should not surprise us. William J. Love was an employee of the IMM concededly controlled by British interests. J. Barston Smull had been with the firm of J. H. Winchester & Co., steamship agents and brokers, directly associated with British shipping. And A. J. Frey was for many years associated with the Pacific Mail Steamship Company, one of the largest British shipping companies.

A careful study of the revelations made by Senator LaFollette in 1921 leads to but one conclusion. American banking and railroad interests organized the IMM to prevent for all time the building of an American-owned, American flag merchant marine.

Clearly, the network of railroads controlled by J. P. Morgan & Co., the Guarantee Trust Co., and the National City Bank would encourage shipment of cargoes on the IMM—British flag ships. The directors of these banks also served as directors of the IMM.

E. C. Grenfell, who was a partner in Morgan, Grenfell and Company of London, was also a director of several British shipping companies controlled by the IMM.

To the extent that railroads can control the cargoes upon which shipping companies rely for the successful operation of their fleets, it is clear that the IMM had a virtual monopoly on available cargoes. Heads of banks financing large networks of railroads did favor the IMM even though the vast majority of the IMM ships flew the British flag.

In the face of such competition, no American flag shipping company could successfully compete. Actually, the organization of the IMM excluded the possibility of establishing an American flag merchant marine.

"The deal" effected between the IMM and the British Board of Trade in 1903 for the operation of the IMM fleet under the British flag and which was renewed in 1910 and 1919, in the writer's opinion, constituted a complete capitulation in the field of shipping by American financiers to Great Britain.

Chapter Seven

SHIPOWNERS BRIBE LEADERS

The disaster suffered by the International Seamen's Union in 1921 must not be laid at the door of the United States Shipping Board in its entirety. The venality and corruption of the leaders of the various autonomous unions of the ISU played an important role. With the outbreak of World War I, the ISU membership jumped by leaps and bounds. After the war, it continued to grow and the union agreements were even improved. Yet the 1921 strike was not only without leadership but also without militancy.

The utter corruption of the ISU leadership in 1921 was unknown at that time. It was not until 1936 when the rank and file members of the Marine Cooks & Stewards Union, ISU, began an action for an accounting against David E. Grange, its president, that corruption was exposed. During this proceeding in the New York Supreme Court, it was shown by sworn affidavits that Henry P. Griffin and Grange, who represented the Cooks and Stewards Union during the 1921 negotiations, were accepting bribes from the steamship companies running as high as $1,225 per month. Seven different steamship companies were named as bribers. Among these companies was included the powerful United Fruit Company.

British trade union leaders, who were not only agents of British shipowners but were also known to collaborate with some of the American maritime union leaders were eager to see American wage scales reduced. British wage rates were nine pounds (a little more than $40) per month for an A.B. and nine pounds, ten shillings ($42) for a fireman.

BRITISH WORKING CONDITIONS

British shipowners at that time were also trying to replace British seamen with lascar* seamen. Out of 200,000 seamen employed in the British Merchant Marine, 52,000 are lascars. After the war, a lascar was being paid two pounds ($9) per month and a fireman two pounds ten shillings ($11) per month.

The working day in the British merchant marine at that time was eight hours a day for the fireman (who worked without rest days), twelve hours for the sailors and fifteen hours for the stewards. The hourly rate was, therefore, much lower than the American.

Ernest Bevin's *Seafarers Record*, official organ of the Transport Workers Union, during the heat of a personal

*An East Indian native sailor.

quarrel with Havelock Wilson, head of the National Union of Seamen, investigated the accommodations for ships' crews. It showed that British prisoners had 800 feet of cubic air space per person while British seamen had to be satisfied with 120 cubic feet per person. In addition, prisoners were provided with blankets, mattresses and the use of baths, while British seamen were not.

The cynical attitude of the leaders of the British seamen is further shown by an editorial in the union's official organ, *The Seaman,* approving the speech of the Australian shipowner representative at the Geneva Labor Conference, a speech which for sheer impudence stands unsurpassed.

The Seaman, on November 6, 1929, discussed it as follows:

We have stated that any alteration in the hours of seamen must be consistent with the best interests of the seamen and the industry by which they live, and that we are not the only people who hold this view is exemplified by the following statement made by the Australian Employers' Delegate at the conference:

Mr. Free (Employers' Delegate, Australia) :

I should first of all like to say a few words about this forty-eight hour week at sea. The query that comes to my mind is, what will the seaman do with his leisure hours when at sea? Will he be happier or more contented? Sixteen hours a day plus twenty-four hours on Sunday amounts to 120 hours a week. A ship at sea is an appalling place for a man who has nothing to do. He cannot walk in the parks or go to the theatre or cinema with his family, as his more fortunate brother employed on shore can do, *and there is just a danger that he may sit and brood over his unhappy lot and his imaginary injustices.* As regards real hard work, compared with the docker, the miner, the navy and the farm labourer, the sailor is not a hard-worked man. On night duty at sea there is one man steering, one man on the look-out and the remainder of the watch standing-by. May it not be a mistake to give him too much leisure at sea?

The NSU did demand the eight-hour workday for officers. Could it be because officers were not likely to brood?

SHIPOWNERS FINANCE UNIONS

The officials of the British National Union of Seamen also had the co-operation of the shipowners in the collection of dues—co-operation which shipowners are usually reluctant to give unless they feel they can control the union. No captain would allow on his ship any person who had not paid his dues up to date. When a union is helpful to shipowners, it appears, they not only do not object to the check-off but actually help its enforcement.

But the British shipowners went even further in the matter of supporting the National Union of Seamen. In 1932, for example, this union's annual expenditures for its upkeep, according to its official organ, *The Seaman,* was given at 127,000 pounds ($571,000). If each seaman's dues were to be paid up a membership of 25,000 seamen, as of 1927, would produce no more than 70,000 pounds ($315,000). The yearly deficit was, therefore, enormous. Where did the money to overcome the deficit come from? The answer is to be found in an item in the union's financial report described as "other incomes." This must be the subsidy from the shipowners for the upkeep of the union.

British shipowners are much more circumspect than American shipowners and get much more for their money.

Instead of giving bribes to union officials directly, they maintained a "company union" which serves them much more effectively. To this day it is the best insurance against effective strikes in the British Merchant Marine.

The wage rates and employment of lascars still prevail. A memorandum of a conference of the All-India Seamen's Federation held in Calcutta in October, 1942, reveals the following:

1. The number of Indian seamen at present employed in the British Mercantile Marine is at least 40,000 or 25 per cent of the ratings of the whole British Mercantile Navy.

2. There had not been an increase in the wages of Indian seamen from 1919 to 1939. By 1939 the average wages of an Indian seaman was 23 rupees (35s). The wages of the Indian seamen after two increases amounts to 5 pounds, 5 shillings ($22.50) per month.

There is no provision for the payment for overtime, and accommodation for those workers is deplorable.

The situation in the British Merchant Marine cannot help but have a direct bearing on present planning for the American Merchant Marine.

Present maritime unions in the United States must concern themselves with the conditions and wages of British seamen. The American Merchant Marine sooner or later will be affected by this situation and the impact of those low wages on the working conditions and wages of American seamen cannot be avoided.

Chapter Eight

RANK AND FILE ORGANIZES

The well advertised open-shop policy ot the ship-owners, which followed in the wake of the 1921 and 1922 seamen's strikes, was by no means restricted to the maritime industry. George Meany, now secretary of the AFL, offered the following explanation for the decline in organization of the AFL in 1924:

Led by the National Association of Manufacturers and the National Metal Trades Association, the open-shop drive was launched by industry which was aided by the economic situation, and an unfriendly attitude towards labor on the part of the Government and the courts.

During the period of prosperity in the twenties, there was no appreciable gain in trade union organization. Between 1925 and 1929 the AFL was almost at a standstill. The lack of organizational activities among the AFL unions during the 1920's left the workers completely unprepared to resist the wholesale wage cuts that ensued with the coming of the depression.

The fact is that when the depression was at its deepest point, with 17,000,000 workers unemployed, thousands of seamen found themselves not only without jobs, but without a union.

Because of the shock and resentment which followed

the sinking of the *SS Vestris* in 1928 merchant seamen in various ports throughout the country began to organize international seamen's clubs. This was the beginning of renewed organization among seamen.

SEAMEN'S CLUBS

These clubs had no affiliation with any national labor organization but constituted meeting places for merchant seamen. Here they could talk freely about their problems without the surveillance of hostile guards and police employed at the Seamen's Church Institute and similar hostelries accommodating seamen in large seaports.

The Seamen's Church Institute and similar institutions in other ports are charitable organizations originally conceived to give aid to helpless seamen. Their funds came primarily from the shipowners. This fact made of them, altogether too often, tools of the shipowners.

It was these seamen's clubs which exposed the campaign launched by the shipowners to whitewash the Lamport and Holt Steamship Company for the extraordinary loss of lives which resulted from the sinking of the *SS Vestris*. These clubs exposed the unseaworthy condition of the ship, its rotten and leaking life boats, and failure of the government inspectors properly to inspect the ship prior to its departure from an American port.

Out of these clubs grew the Marine Workers Progressive League, forerunner of the Marine Workers Industrial Union.

Meanwhile, an energetic campaign was launched against the racketeering of the Seamen's Institute and the two-watch system which was being forced upon crews of most ships, despite the provisions of the Seamen's Act. The blacklist system also became the center of many struggles and activities at this time. These campaigns were carried on both on board ships and ashore.

THE HUNGER MARCH

At the height of the depression, when workers throughout the land were undergoing horrible hardships, the sufferings of the merchant seamen could not bear description. Homeless during the most prosperous periods, many became complete derelicts during the depression. And yet, in spite of the privations to which they were exposed, an experience of the writer during the November, 1932 hunger march suggested the tremendous feeling of confidence that the workers had in the strength and the militancy of the merchant seamen.

Several thousand hunger marchers were gathered at Union Square in New York, from which point the hunger march was to begin. At about ten o'clock in the morning the crowd became restless and yet were not quite ready to march. About that time, off in the distance, the sharp notes of fife and drum corps could be heard. This fife and drum corps led the delegation of marching seamen who were coming to the square from South Ferry.

The awareness on the part of the marchers that the seamen, designated as the leaders of the march, had come to join them electrified the entire seething mass of somewhat frightened workers. The fearlessness of the seamen had impressed itself upon the unemployed during the previous year and the change in the animation of the crowded square was understandable.

CALL TO MARITIME WORKERS

In the meantime, on April 27, 1930, the Marine Workers Progressive League met and reorganized as the Marine

Workers Industrial Union. It issued a call to all seamen, longshoremen, and harbor workers. Every member of the MWIU considered himself a union organizer and demanded that ships' committees be organized and that the union be brought on board the ships. Conditions were rotten, but the only way to change them, the MWIU argued, was to organize, organize, and organize. Growling in the foc's'le or messroom and the quitting of ships was discouraged. Seamen were urged not to wait for "better times," but were urged to improve conditions. If the crews on board ships were to continue to do nothing, the only result would be that conditions would grow worse and the pay lower.

Each ship was urged not to wait until the next ship starts action or until all of the ships are organized. If the food was rotten, slop chest prices high, and no night lunch—then a committee should be organized and sent to the captain to demand a change. If the ship was short-handed, a committee should be organized to call upon the Steamboat Inspector and demand that a full crew be signed on. If the wages on board the ships were being cut, the alternative was not to quit but rather to stay on the ship and refuse to work until the old scale was paid and until the three-watch system was established.

On December 5, 1930, a delegation of ten from the MWIU in New York arrived in Washington and attempted to see President Hoover to place before him a petition. President Hoover, of course, found no time for them. In any event they left the petition at the White House. This petition contained the following demands:

1. All seamen unemployed for one month or longer to receive $1 a day during period of unemployment. This sum to be raised from funds now appropriated, through the Jones-

White Act, for direct subsidies and loans to the shipowners. All funds appropriated to be distributed under the supervision of committees elected by the seamen. Relief to be granted all seamen sailing on American ships regardless of nationality.

2. Unemployed seamen to be allowed the right of admittance to all Marine Hospitals regardless of length of time ashore. All dental and optical work to be free.

3. Full enforcement of manning scale; three watches on all ships; no workaways or forced labor on any ships.

4. Immediate abolition of the blacklist and deferred lists and logging systems.

5. Establishments of Central Shipping Bureaus in all ports under the supervision of elected committees of seamen.

6. Laid-up ships to be requisitioned and fitted up as lodging for unemployed seamen.

7. Passage of the Workers Unemployment Insurance Bill.

The period between 1931 and 1933 was the first period in which merchant seamen engaged in a struggle against their employers. The International Seamen's Union was almost extinct for ten years and the activities of the Marine Workers Indusrial Union, when analyzed in retrospect, were almost spontaneous acts by merchant seamen.

During the early days, the MWIU organized a whole series of actions to prevent the worsening of conditions and the lowering of wages. With the organization of the MWIU came spontaneous action on ships of various operators. On Munson Line vessels alone, as many as thirty ships' crews took action against the horrible conditions which existed on the vessels operated by that company.

By 1933, the policy of the MWIU changed from one of fighting against the worsening of conditions into one of demanding higher wages and better conditions.

President Roosevelt had already been elected. During this time the militancy of the workers was developing. The *Diamond Cement* was tied to its dock in the port of Baltimore and the crew engaged in what perhaps was the first sit-down strike in America. They demanded higher wages and improvement in living conditions. The entire Baltimore waterfront was galvanized into action. A scab crew from New York was prevented from boarding the ship and, upon its arrival, joined the striking crew.

The vessel did leave the port with a skeleton scab crew and upon its arrival in Philadelphia, and thereafter in New York, was met with militant action at each port.

Finally, the company, in despair, capitulated and granted all of the original demands made in the port of Baltimore. The organization of the Central Bureau of Shipping in the port of Baltimore, which will be discussed in succeeding chapters, was set in motion by the militancy of the marine workers in this situation.

The Marine Workers Industrial Union agent in the port of Baltimore at that time was Al Lannon. Mr. Lannon, who was to become one of the leaders of the 1936-37 East Coast strike, was the leader of the *Diamond Cement* strike.

Between 1930 and 1934, the Marine Workers Industrial Union organized branches in almost every important port in the United States. It not only endeavored to organize the seagoing marine workers, but made heroic attempts in an effort to organize longshoremen. An illustration of their effectiveness among the longshoremen is the support they gave to the 1932 strike among the coastwise longshoremen during that year.

The *Marine Worker's Voice* was the official organ of

the Marine Workers Industrial Union. A copy of this paper found its way to the docks in the port of Norfolk. Influenced by the paper three hundred longshoremen in that port met and organized a local and sent delegates to represent the Norfolk longshoremen at the 1933 convention of the MWIU which was held in the port of New York.

The effectiveness of the MWIU resulted in a vicious campaign of terror against its organizers and officials in the various ports where branches were maintained. In San Pedro, where the red squads were most vicious, the union offices were smashed and the officials were forced to carry on their activities secretly.

Chapter Nine

SEAMEN AND THE NEW DEAL

Immediately after his inauguration on March 4, 1933, President Roosevelt addressed Congress on the need of enacting a recovery program. Conditions prevailing in our land at that time were poignantly described by the President as follows:

In such a spirit on my part and on yours we face our common difficulties. They concern, thank God, only material things. Values have shrunken to fantastic levels; taxes have risen; our ability to pay has fallen; government of all kinds is faced by serious curtailment of income; the means of exchange are frozen in the currents of trade; the withered leaves of industrial enterprise lie on every side; farmers find no market for their produce; the savings of many years in thousands of families are gone.

More important, a host of unemployed citizens face the grim problem of existence, and an equally great number toil with little return. Only a foolish optimist can deny the dark realities of the moment.

The President proposed immediate enrollment of unemployed workers for such public employment as could be immediately started. He further proposed that Congress immediately make appropriations for the purpose of grants to the states for relief work and the immediate establishment of a broad public works labor-creating program.

In order to reorganize the economic structure in our land after the banks had been closed, the National Industrial Recovery Act was passed. Codes of Fair Competition were to be formulated for all industries. Industries in which workers were highly organized, such as the needle trades, building trades, etc., obtained rather substantial gains in the Codes. For instance, the International Ladies' Garment Workers Union secured a 35-hour, 5-day week, with wage increases to make up for loss in hours.

NO ORGANIZATION

The maritime industry, however, had no organization whatsoever. The shipowners, seeking to freeze the low wages and the deplorable working conditions then prevalent, agreed to hearings on a shipping code. The hearings were held in Washington in November, 1933.

International Seamen's Union officials, having abandoned the unorganized completely, suddenly came into the picture and offered to collaborate with the shipowners in the establishment of a Maritime Labor Board. The board was to be composed of representatives of shipowners and representatives of the sailors', firemen's and cooks' division of the ISU.

An MWIU committee, headed by Roy Hudson, appeared at the hearings to oppose shipowner proposals and submit recommendations of their own. The union objected to legal endorsement of the 12-hour day for seamen, which at that time was prevailing on almost 50 per cent of American ships. It objected, also, to the fact that no provision was made for the payment of overtime, and more particularly, the failure of the Code to preserve the right of the seamen to strike.

Reminding the shipowners that the purpose of the Code was to improve the conditions in the industry, the spokesman for the Marine Workers Industrial Union cited the following wage rates:

On the Grace Line, $50 for ABs, $30 for ordinary seamen, boatswain $58, carpenters $63, firemen $50, wipers $30, boiler tenders $52, oilers $50 and Chinese stewards $25.

The Moore McCormack Steamship Company pay firemen $40, oilers $45, watertenders $47.50, ABs $40, ordinary seamen $25 a month.

On the Munson Line, the wages for able bodied seamen are $37.50 a month, firemen $35, wipers $22.50, oilers $25, and watertenders $47.50.

Not only were the ships at that time being operated by crews that were underpaid, but they were also actually undermanned. Unemployed seamen, under the threat of starvation as a result of unemployment, were compelled to take jobs for which they received little more than their meals and a place to sleep. The food that was being served to these workers was aptly described by a member of the crew of the *Mundixie* as follows: "We had stew for twenty-one consecutive nights, and the coffee was warmed over from the officers' mess, and the bread stale and soggy." Food on this ship was in no way different from that on most other American ships during that period.

MWIU PROPOSALS

The MWIU presented at the Code hearings not only wage demands for the offshore industries, but made concrete proposals for the improvement of conditions of longshoremen and Inland Waterway workers as well as the seamen employed on the Great Lakes. The delegation proposed:

1. That the industry and the government assume the responsibility for one fixed weekly and yearly wage for every worker in the industry, this to be guaranteed by providing that no worker shall receive less than forty (40) weeks work per year.

2. Hours of labor shall not be more than eight (8) hours per day or 44 per week. There shall not be less than three watches for those workers employed in the propulsion and navigation of the vessel. Where watches are required on Sunday and holidays for safety and navigation only of vessel at sea, equal time off for all labor in excess of forty-four hours shall be given at full wages at the first port of call; or in lieu of this overtime rates shall be paid.

3. Wages shall be set at the minimum rate provided for in the 1930 U. S. Shipping Scale, which as a result of a guaranteed working week will provide a minimum yearly wage for every category of worker (for example, $625 minimum yearly wage for an AB at USSB scale of $62.50 per month) .

4. On all vessels carrying dangerous, inflammable and

obnoxious cargo (oil tankers, sulphur-boats, munitions, etc.) an additional increase of 20 per cent in wages shall be given. All work performed in excess of eight (8) hours per day shall be paid for at overtime rates of 75 cents per hour for unlicensed men and $1.25 for licensed men.

5. Wages shall be adjusted monthly as prices rise so that there will be no lowering of the living standards due to inflation. Seamen shall be entitled to full payment of wages upon demand in any port and to payment in gold in foreign ports.

6. Where industry does not provide a worker with this minimum yearly earning the government shall pay government unemployment insurance equal to this amount. For workers not totally unemployed the difference between actual earnings and the minimum wage shall be paid out of government unemployment insurance.

To make funds immediately available for this purpose all funds now used for subsidies, shipbuilding loans, etc., as provided under the 1928 Merchant Marine (Jones-White) Act shall be appropriated.

7. Equal pay for equal work regardless of race, nationality, age or sex. No member of the crew shall be required to do work other than they are signed on for (OSs are not to do AB's work. Seamen are not to do longshoremen's work).

Foreign born and Negro seamen have the right to any job without discrimination.

8. There shall be no blacklisting nor logging. A seaman shall be eligible to all civic rights of other workers. All seamen including Asiatic seamen shall be entitled to go ashore in any port.

9. The present U. S. Shipping Board scale of manning shall be increased 33 1/3 per cent. This shall be considered the minimum manning scale on all ships.

Full wages shall be paid for every member of the crew and there shall be a complete abolition of the workaway system.

10. Food shall be of adequate quality and quantity suitable

to climate and weather conditions and subject to inspection of ships' committee.

A minimum of 60 cents per man, per day, ration allowance shall be provided. This is to be increased as the cost of living rises. Fifty cents a meal shall be allowed when vessel does not feed. Fifteen minutes rest period shall be allowed for each watch and twice per day during the morning and afternoon for day men. Night lunches shall be provided.

Adequate washing facilities, including washing buckets, showers and fresh water, shall be provided and clean linen, soap and matches shall be supplied weekly.

11. Fink halls and shipping masters shall be abolished and a central shipping agency with a rotary system of engagement under control of elected committees of seamen shall be instituted.

12. When a seaman is discharged in any port other than his home port, he shall be entitled to full transportation home at full rates of pay. All seamen regardless of time ashore shall be entitled to free hospitalization.

The workers shall have the right to belong to any union of their own choosing and the right to strike whenever the workers' demands are not otherwise granted.

The Seamen's Code shall provide recognition of democratically elected committees of the seamen representatives of all departments on a vessel.

These ship committees to be recognized by the employers in the enforcement of wages, hours, discharges and conditions of labor contained in the above provisions and any other problems that may arise.

Naturally, these proposals were ignored.

In case anyone thinks the committee's description of conditions was exaggerated, let me quote from a report of the newly formed Maritime Commission, November 10, 1937. Discussing the industry in the early 1930s, the report said:

Wages fell and working conditions grew steadily worse until, at the depth of the depression, some American seamen were receiving as little as $25 a month, living under wretched conditions, eating unpalatable food, and working 12 hours or more a day. . . .

Some of the operators who paid low wages during the depression were at the same time receiving substantial subsidies from the Government for the preservation of an American standard of living.

THE CENTRALIZED SHIPPING BUREAU

In February, 1934, the MWIU called a mass meeting of all the seamen on the beach in Baltimore. More than 700 seamen appeared. It was agreed to establish a Centralized Shipping Bureau (CBS) for the port of Baltimore, to do away with all favoritism, blacklisting, and discrimination. At this meeting MWIU leaders pointed out that for the CSB to become a success it must be the property of all the seamen, regardless of what union or organization they belonged to, and that all the rules must be approved by the membership before they became effective. A committee of seamen was elected to carry out the following decisions:

1. That all seamen pledge not to ship through any other place but the CSB.

2. That the committee visit all the crimps and tell them that from that date they are to ship their men from CSB or be boycotted.

3. That all shipping is to be done on a rotary system.

4. That all men register according to their ratings.

5. That the man at the top of the list be given three chances to ship and if he refuses the third job he is to go to the bottom of the list.

6. That when a man takes the first standby job it should

be counted as a regular job regardless of how many days he works.

7. That all grievances be taken up at the meetings and the body vote on them.

8. That a meeting is to be held at least once a week.

9. That the Centralized Shipping Bureau is not to ship any men on any ship that is on strike or has any other labor dispute.

The Centralized Shipping Bureau was to be controlled entirely by a United Front Shipping Committee. The reasons for its establishment were very well set forth in a report by Harry Alexander, chairman of the committee which established the Baltimore Centralized Shipping Bureau. I quote from one of his reports:

The seamen have been for years the prey of all sorts of parasites. Every time a ship docks (no matter at what port or what country) it doesn't take long for the ship to be filled with all sorts of merchants, tailors, bootleggers, boarding house keepers, barbers, shoemakers, prostitutes, and agents for prostitutes. All these parasites are allowed aboard the ships, but when a seaman tries to board a ship to look for a job or get a meal he will be promptly chased off, and these parasites have the run of the ship.

But of all these parasites the shipping agent is the most ruthless. He does not even go aboard the ships; he knows that the seamen will eventually come to him to look for a job. These shipping agents (crimps, as we will call them from now on), who are useless as far as the seamen are concerned, are given the power by the shipowners to dictate to the seamen as to who is to go on a certain job.

These crimps are not satisfied with what they are getting from the shipowners for shipping men. They have various sidelines. Most of them have rooming houses where they charge the seamen from three to five dollars a week and then in some cases put from three to six in one room. Others have cheap restaurants where the seamen have to pay first-class prices for third-class food; some have clothing stores where the seamen are forced to pay 35 and 40 dollars for a suit of clothes, for which any decent place would charge 15 or 16 dollars; and then there are some who have saloons either in their name or in somebody else's, where the seamen are forced to spend their money in order to get a job.

The seamen in every port of the United States, with the exception of Baltimore where the Centralized Shipping Bureau is in power, are forced to patronize these places in order to get a job on a ship and then he is only able to get a job in one company, because he would have to stay in every crimp joint on the waterfront to be able to sail on all company ships.

CSB IMPROVES CONDITIONS

Shipowners dealt with shipping crimps because it enabled them to keep the merchant seamen in virtual slavery. Each crimp became actually the agent for a particular shipping operator. When the rank and file in Baltimore set up the CSB, the shipowners avoided that port as much as possible. Conditions on ships that sailed out of Baltimore grew better, wages were raised (in some cases by $15 a month), and men were added to the crew. The seamen who were blacklisted and discriminated against in other ports began to drift into Baltimore and in less than six weeks there were over 1300 men registered in the CSB.

But even though the CSB was successful in increasing wages and improving conditions, its most important contribution to the well being of the seamen was the complete abolition of discrimination against Negroes and Filipinos. The Bureau afforded the same rights of shipping to Negroes, Filipinos, and other nationals that it guaranteed to the white seamen. The Bureau soon enough recognized that if they were not to accord equal rights to the Negroes with those of other seamen, the Bureau could not have lasted a week. The shipowners would have smashed the Bureau by boycotting it and hiring those seamen who had been discriminated against by the Bureau.

Soon the operators began to realize that if they wanted their ships to sail, they would have to improve conditions and raise the wages. Crews on many ships, however, were forced to strike. There were more than fifty strikes by individual ship unions in the port of Baltimore in less than two months. The solidarity of the crews on the ships and the men on the beach were unshakable; no matter what the strikers' demands were, they included recognition of the CSB.

The success of the Baltimore men in improving their conditions gradually became known in all ports along the Atlantic Coast. It was on the lips of every seaman and became common talk in every mess hall. Seamen could not congregate in any restaurant or union hall without discussing the Baltimore project. The success of the Baltimore Shipping Bureau was in no small measure responsible for the intensity of the struggle of the West Coast seamen who were already preparing for the 1934 strike—the strike which ultimately emancipated them from the plague of the shipping crimps.

The Centralized Shipping Bureau was finally smashed by the intervention of the government on the side of the shipowners. Relief was refused to the seamen who were housed in a project which was under the supervision and management of the Centralized Shipping Bureau. The absence of similar conditions in ports along the Atlantic made it impossible for Baltimore to continue its Bureau.

While the shipowners and the government succeeded in smashing this novel undertaking on the part of the seamen, it did serve as a lesson and inspiration to some maritime workers and laid the foundations for the great struggle of 1934.

Chapter Ten

THE 1934 STRIKE

The 1921 seamen's strike had been preceded, in 1919, by no less disastrous a strike among the Pacific longshoremen. It was broken with considerable violence. Strikebreakers were employed and the whole machinery of government was used to smash the strike. The longshoremen unfortunately were alone in this fight. Neither the ISU nor the Teamsters Union, both affiliates of the AFL, gave the longshoremen any assistance. The failure of the seamen to assist the longshoremen was, of course, responsible for the unwillingness of the longshoremen to give the seamen any assistance whatsoever two years later.

With the San Francisco Local of the International Longshoremen's Association completely smashed, an independent Longshoremen's Association known as the Blue Book Union came into existence. It was clearly a company union, completely under the control of the employers. Longshoremen could not secure employment on the West Coast waterfronts unless they were members of it.

The "contract" between the employers and the Blue Book Union contained a closed shop provision inserted by the shipowners. Since the union was under their complete control, this is understandable. This did not, of course, mean that the wages were increased. As a matter of fact, between 1927 and 1929 some longshoremen earned less than $10 a week. True, the great majority earned a little more than that. The favored gangs were the only longshoremen that earned anything like a living wage.

For four years, beginning in 1930, the Marine Workers Industrial Union, which had branches in the important ports on the West Coast as well as on the East Coast, hammered away on the question of union control of hiring. A shape-up requiring longshoremen to be hired twice a day had become the horrible nightmare of every longshoreman who worked for a living.*

MWIU DEMANDS

The program of the MWIU included demands for all marine workers. They were in effect:

1. Full recognition of hiring only through union halls,

*Between 1920 and 1923 the writer was employed intermittently on the docks in New York and had personal experience with the shape-up. Picture a longshoreman leaving Brooklyn at four o'clock in the morning to get to a dock in Staten Island at six-thirty to make the shape-up, not chosen for a job and returning to his home several hours later. One should observe the pallor that spreads over a worker's face when, after standing in the snow and sleet for an hour before the shape-up, he finds himself without a day's work! That nightmare, by the way, still prevails on the East Coast.

no men to be hired on dock or street or through shipping masters, complete recognition of ship and dock committees.

2. Abolition of all fink halls and of sea service bureaus (this was a bureau established by the Shipping Board as a government hiring hall).

3. No discrimination on account of race, creed, or color.

4. Full political, social, and economic equality for whites, Negroes, and Asiatics.

Demands for seamen included a scale of wages equal at least to that of 1920 (which provided $85.00 a month for able-bodied seamen), the same food for crew as for officers, three watches on deck, four watches in engine room of coal burners, abolition of fines and logging, eight hours a day for stewards' department, all overtime to be paid at the rate of 75 cents an hour with Sunday and holiday work to be classed as overtime.

Demands for longshoremen included the restoration of the 1919 wage scale of $1 an hour with double pay for dangerous and special cargo, double time for overtime, no man to work more than sixteen hours without eight hours rest, larger gangs and not less than eight men in the hold at any time. Dock committees were to be established to see that all these conditions were enforced and no ship was to work unless these dock committees approved the condition of the gear and rigging.

In the summer of 1933 a charter was issued to a group of the San Francisco longshoremen by the ILA. This was an attempt to restore the power of the old line ILA officials among the longshoremen who were beginning to rebel against the Blue Book company union. But the militancy of the rank and file was such that during the latter part of 1933 and the early part of 1934 a break between them seemed imminent. Organizing committees were formed by the rank and file and union strength rose.

During that period the leadership of Harry Bridges began. Among the rank and file demands was that of a dispatching hall under the joint management of the union and the employer. Negotiations between the union and the employers, which began in the spring of 1934, broke down on May 1. On May 7 the longshoremen unanimously voted to strike and stopped work two days later.

FOR INDUSTRIAL ORGANIZATION

The program of the MWIU formulated at its convention in 1930 specifically provided for organization of all maritime workers on an industrial basis. It was, therefore, natural that the MWIU would support the longshoremen. When the strike began the MWIU called meetings of the crews of ships lying in San Francisco ports. A conference of delegates of ships was held and voted that the MWIU support the strike wholeheartedly.

ISU crews, too, struck and marched to their union halls to register for strike duty. ISU officials advised these crews not to strike and return to their ships. Instead of returning to their ships they marched down to the MWIU halls and registered there. In order to prevent wholesale registrations of the striking seamen at the MWIU halls, the ISU was compelled to issue its own strike call within about ten days after the longshoremen went on strike.

The support of the longshoremen, however, was not restricted to seamen. Teamsters who carried cargo to and from the waterfront also supported the longshoremen.

Ten unions, in all, joined the strike. They were: International Longshoremen's Association West Coast locals; three craft unions of the ISU on the West Coast; Sailors' Union of the Pacific of the ISU; Marine Cooks & Stewards Union of the ISU; Marine Firemen, Oilers, Watertenders and Wipers of the ISU; Marine Engineers Beneficial Association; Masters, Mates & Pilots; American Radio Telegraphists; Inland Boatmen's Union; and Ship Clerk's Association.

Finally, as a means of co-ordinating the activities of all of the striking unions, a Joint Strike Committee was set up. This committee was controlled by the rank and file under the leadership of Harry Bridges.

WEST COAST LEADERSHIP

One of the things that stood out most in the minds of all West Coast workers was the effectiveness and the clearsightedness of the new leadership. The members of the Joint Strike Committee were elected from among the rank and file at regular union meetings. Nominations were regularly made at one meeting and at succeeding meetings elections took place. The union constitution made no provision for such a committee. But its effectiveness was so apparent and the support it received from the rank and file was so obvious that no one dared challenge its authority.

ISU and ILA officials, as well as the ship operators, became truly alarmed by the effectiveness of the Joint Strike Committee. The employers instituted their usual anti-red campaign—except that it was completely unrestrained. The police became more aggressive. The MWIU hall was raided. A "back-to-work" movement was organized by the repudiated AFL officials during the early part of June. On June 16 an agreement was signed in the office of Mayor Rossi of San Francisco with ILA President Joseph P. Ryan, one of the signers. This agreement was signed without having been submitted to the membership for ratification and notice of its acceptance was sent to the newspapers before the membership was notified. This sell out was rejected by the membership.

STRIKE CONTINUES

This failure on the part of the government officials and the AFL officials to bring the strike to an end impelled the shipowners, through their Industrial Association, to issue an announcement that they intended to open the port. Governor Merriam is reported to have stated:

If the state cannot settle through negotiations, I shall take steps to enforce the issue and open up state property on the waterfront to the resumption of commerce.

On July 5, the Industrial Association mobilized strike-breakers and with the support of the police and the National Guard, which was already on duty, an attack was made upon the picket line which resulted in a free for all on the Embarcadero. When the skirmish was over, one striker was dead and one died later.

Instead of frightening the strikers, the death of these two longshoremen aroused greater feelings for unity among the longshoremen. The two strikers who had been killed during the fight lay in state at the longshoremen's headquarters. Men and women from all over the city brought flowers into the headquarters. Wreaths were also placed on the spot where the longshoremen had been shot. When a policeman took it upon himself to kick the flowers from the spot where they had been placed by sympathizers, the spontaneous protest on the part of all the passersby was such that he immediately replaced them.

On July 11 the teamsters voted unanimously to support the maritime unions. Promptly thereafter the butchers, boilermakers, taxi drivers, the painters and machinists followed suit. A general strike was called. By July 13, more than 32,000 union members were on strike.

The San Francisco general strike electrified labor from coast to coast. Employers saw in it the "seed of revolution." Newspaper editorial writers wrote reams on "anarchy" and the need for "law and order."

The attack on the militant workers was intensified. Red-baiting by press, radio, and public officials became so great that the Central Labor Council voted to call off the general strike. This, in effect, was a capitulation by the old line AFL officials to the pressure of the Waterfront Employer Associations. This did not mean that support for the marine strikers had completely waned. The chairman of the meeting counted 191 votes in favor of calling off the strike and 174 against it.

RANKS HOLD

The calling off of the general strike by the officials of the Central Labor Council, however, did not break the ranks of the striking maritime workers. The strike continued until finally a coastwise vote was taken on the question of submitting the dispute to arbitration. It passed and on July 31 the seamen began to return to work, followed soon by the longshoremen. The dispute was submitted to arbitration and on October 12, 1934, the National Longshoremen's Board handed down its award providing for the longshoremen:

1. *Hiring:* Joint control of a hiring hall by the employers

and the ILA, cost evenly divided, with an ILA dispatcher. No discrimination in the employment of longshoremen, whether union or non-union.

2. *Hours:* The 5-day, 30-hour week; 6-hour day.

3. *Wages:* 95½ cents per hour for straight time; $1.40 per hour for overtime, and overtime was described as any time worked in excess of six hours between 8 AM and 5 PM, and during meal time, on weekdays; between 5 PM Saturday and 8 AM Monday; and on legal holidays. There was also provision for handling obnoxious, dangerous and damaged cargo, and the establishment of a Labor Relations Committee for the handling of alleged wage and other abuses.

4. *Labor Relations Committee:* A board of six men, three from the employers and three from the ILA.

Throughout the strike, the operators had taken the position that they could not bargain with the unions of the seagoing personnel. The relative strength of the MWIU and the SIU was about equal and the employers had taken the position that they could not recognize one as against the other. As a matter of fact, the shipowners were doing nothing but stalling, hoping that they would not be obliged to recognize any union.

The effectiveness of the MWIU, however, became apparent to the shipowners throughout the country when, on June 2, right in the heat of the strike, the MWIU succeeded in striking the *SS Texan,* a West Coast ship, while she was lying at a dock in the port of New York. Twenty-two out of a crew of twenty-nine left the ship in support of the West Coast strike.

ISU officials attempted to break up the picket line around the *SS Texan* and before the day was over succeeded in having several pickets arrested. That night the

ISU officials in New York furnished a crew to the *SS Texan.*

ISU officials at the West Coast convinced the shipowners on both the East Coast and the West Coast that much would be gained by the latter if they undertook negotiations with them. It should be remembered that between 1922 and 1934 ISU officials engaged in no organizational activity among the unorganized.

On the East Coast, the officials and members of the MWIU did everything in their power to mobilize support for the West Coast strike. This was, in every instance, sabotaged and frustrated by the officials of the International Seamen's Union who were beginning to creep out of their holes at that time to exert whatever influence they could against the extension of the strike.

ANDREW FURUSETH

It should be made clear at this point, that, in the author's condemnation of corrupt ISU officialdom, he always exempts that great leader, Andrew Furuseth, one of the truly heroic figures in the early maritime labor picture.

Furuseth was Norwegian by birth and had followed the sea from early manhood. He came to America in the 1880's, settled in San Francisco, and joined the Coast Seamen's Union. From that time on, his life was devoted to the building of the union and the betterment of working conditions on ships.

Even after he became president of the International Seamen's Union—a post he held the better part of his life—he eschewed personal comforts because seamen did not enjoy them on ships. During his long years in Washington, he lived in a furnished room, ate plain meals, and was content to lead a simple life.

The late Senator Robert M. LaFollette gave Furuseth credit for passage of the Seamen's (LaFollette) Act of 1915, a measure for which Furuseth labored unceasingly for twenty years.

It was not until the 1920's, by which time less principled men had wormed their way into ISU leadership, that Furuseth's influence in the union waned. In his old age, he was induced to rail at "the radicals," as the militant rank-and-file was called, and to support the Carlsons, Granges, Hunters, and Scharrenburgs. However, until his death in 1938, at the age of 84, Andrew Furuseth remained in the eyes of American seamen a symbol of their bitter struggles against the inhuman working and living conditions at sea.

While Andrew Furuseth made an extraordinary contribution in the field of obtaining legislation which enfranchised merchant seamen, giving them civil rights enjoyed for decades by other workers, he did not always play a progressive role in the field of organization.

It is a fact that during World War I, and for some time thereafter, he collaborated with the shipowners and the United States Shipping Board to drive militant American and alien seamen from Shipping Board ships.

Chapter Eleven

EAST COAST MOVES

Meanwhile, on the East Coast, under the leadership of the MWIU, a Joint Strike Committee was organized by the rank and file of the ISU and officials of other marine unions. On this committee were represented almost all of the maritime unions with the exception of the ISU. The committee issued a strike call for October 8, 1934. However, it was sabotaged by officials of the ISU Atlantic and Gulf districts and had to be withdrawn, although strike action was taken by about 18 ships' crews.

This militancy of the seamen on the East Coast frightened the shipowners. During December the American Shipowners Association and the Employers Association of the Pacific recognized that their interests would be served best by the signing of an agreement under which they recognized the ISU. They were able to check union control of hiring by granting a preference and hiring clause which read as follows:

It is understood and agreed that, as vacancies occur, members of the ISU of America, who are citizens of the United States, shall be given preference of employment, if they can satisfactorily qualify to fill the respective positions; provided, however, that this section shall not be construed to require the discharge of any employee who may not desire to join the Union, or to apply to prompt reshipment, or absence due to illness or accident.

This foresight on the part of the shipowners and the dispatch with which they acted proved to be quite an advantage to them in the succeeding two years.

Immediately following the calling off of the October 8 strike, a unity conference was called by the MWIU to take place in Boston. The American Radio Telegraphists Association, the MWIU, and various locals of the ILA responded. Delegates were elected directly from some ships and docks.

The conference called upon all local bodies of other unions to discuss proposed demands for seamen, long-shoremen, and radio operators.

In the port of New York a meeting of elected delegates of almost all the maritime unions, with the exception of the ISU, met in a conference to discuss the advisability of calling an East Coast maritime strike. The submission of the West Coast unions of their demands to arbitration and the general attack of the shipowners made it inadvisable to call a maritime strike on the East Coast, although the revolt of the East Coast seamen against their miserable conditions on East Coast ships was taking on momentum.

MWIU PROPOSES UNITY

In November, 1934, an open letter was written to the members of the ISU by the National Committee of the MWIU on the question of unity. This letter reads:

Brothers:
The Marine Workers Industrial Union wishes to speak to you again on the question of unity.

We ask you to consider the following question—is the *International Seamen's Union strong enough to defend the interests of its own members?* The answer can only be—no union in the industry is powerful enough to defeat *all* the shipowners singlehanded.

What is to be done? The Marine Workers Industrial Union has always maintained that united action of the membership of all unions, in defense of common interests, would also rally the unorganized for action, and give us the strength necessary to compel the shipowners to deal with the rank and file seamen and meet our demands for higher wages and better conditions.

Your officials have always opposed such a policy. They incite you against the membership of the Marine Workers Industrial Union in order to prevent united action.

Where does this opposition to a united front lead to? Is it converting the International Seamen's Union into a strike-breaking organization and a company union? Can any one deny that Brown, Olander and other ISU officials were the ones who openly provided scabs to replace the crews who came out on October 8! Remember, too, brothers, that these striking crews included rank and file members of the ISU, who were replaced by scabs recruited by their own officials!

The ISU officials charge that the Marine Workers Industrial Union wants to destroy your organization. We answer —it is the strikebreaking activities of Olander, Scharrenburg, Furuseth and Co., that daily discredit the ISU and disgust many seamen with unionism. The anti-working class activities of these gentlemen are responsible for there being more than one union in the industry. Control of the various unions by the rank and file would result in united action in all our struggles and eventually the amalgamation of all seamen into one union.

It is necessary to speak frankly about these questions

because these officials have recently helped the shipowners betray the seamen, first on the West Coast and now on the East. We know that these defeats will not prevent us from continuing the struggle for higher wages and better conditions and the right to organize. But we must learn from our experience—that only united action will bring victory! In the future as in the past the Marine Workers Industrial Union will do everything possible to help create such unity. We hope that this letter will serve to convince you of this fact and of the necessity for you, upon your part, to carry on a fight against all those who stand against unity and control of your organization by the rank and file.

NEW AGREEMENT SIGNED

With the execution of a new agreement on the East Coast, the shipowners gave complete recognition and control of hiring to ISU officials. In its November call for unity, the MWIU had appealed to the members of the ISU to join with them in the organization of one union, controlled by the rank and file and devoted to the principle of union control of hiring. This call was largely responsible for the decision of the shipowners to enter into the agreement with the old line ISU officials. The execution of the East Coast agreement, therefore, convinced the MWIU National Committee that only unity of all maritime workers would make possible the ultimate attainment of better conditions, higher wages, and union control of hiring.

On December 27, after the East Coast officials signed their agreement with the shipowners, the MWIU stated that if the ISU would agree to submit the Eastern and Gulf Agreement to all of the seamen, the MWIU would agree to merge with the ISU. By recognizing only one of the unions, the shipowners were hoping to keep the workers divided. Since the shipowners controlled the ISU officials they also maintained control of hiring. And they had the blacklist.

The MWIU offered to merge with the ISU upon the following terms:

1. Good standing members of the MWIU to have the same status in the ISU, through the exchange of membership books.

2. A guarantee of trade union democracy, which means the right of all members to express and to fight for their opinions, and the right of election to all positions and the officials of the union to be responsible to the membership.

These proposals were rejected by the ISU officials. By rejecting the majority proposals of the MWIU, the ISU leadership hoped to keep the militants out of the ISU and in this way maintain their union control. They also hoped to be able to drive these militant workers out of the maritime industry.

To defeat this move, the MWIU decided to dissolve and carry through the merger from below in spite of the ISU officialdom. Whereupon, the following March, the MWIU National Committee called upon all seamen not members of the ISU, whether unorganized or members of the MWIU, to join the ISU and build it "into a powerful union." From then on, ISU ranks swelled month by month.

The ISU rank and file in all the ports along the coast in the spring of 1936, under the leadership of former MWIU members, began to demand that membership meetings be held regularly and that all hiring of new crews be done through the union hall. Resolutions to that effect were introduced at meetings of the three ISU component craft unions: the Eastern and Gulf Sailors Association; the Marine Firemen, Oilers and Water-tenders Union; and the Marine Cooks and Stewards of the Atlantic and Gulf.

Unfortunately, the new members that joined the union during the early part of the year had voice but no vote. Membership meetings were, therefore, controlled by union delegates all of whom were appointees of the officials.

Officials of the union were also charged with refusing to organize Filipino, Negro, and foreign-born seamen sailing on American ships. Shipowners wanted these people excluded from unions in order that they might be used as scabs during strikes.

FIRST EAST COAST STRIKE

The first important strike on the East Coast took place in the spring of 1935 in the port of Philadelphia. The *SS Dora* was struck by the rank and file. The movement to organize all ships and build the ISU swept the water-front. Twenty-four hour picket lines were established at all crimps and shipping offices. All seamen were registered for shipping through the union hall, with an elected rank and file committee in charge. Ships that failed to hire through the union hall faced the threat of strike action. Within one week, sixty seamen shipped out of the union hall. Hundreds of seamen joined the union.

Soon the movement spread to other Atlantic and Gulf ports. Sentiment grew for the calling of a conference to discuss the organization of a Marine Federation, similar to that being set up on the Pacific Coast. But this movement was scotched. President Gus Brown of the Eastern and Gulf Association, President David E. Grange of the

Marine Cooks Association, and President Oscar Carlson of the Marine Firemen, Oilers and Watertenders Union descended on the union hall and, protected by thugs, called a meeting and expelled the entire leadership of the port of Philadelphia. The day following their arrival, they called another meeting and dissolved the shipping committee and declared the boycott off on the shipping crimps. Everything that the seamen had accomplished organizationally was ruthlessly torn down by the officials of their own union.

To protect themselves against the rank and file, officials of the Marine Firemen, Oilers and Watertenders Union amended their constitution. The purpose, of course, was to give complete authority to the executive board of the union and to empower them to expel all militant rank and file unions.

Rank and filers applied to the courts for an injunction to halt the change. The injunction was denied. But the trial, because it exposed the scheme to deliver control of the union to an executive board of eleven, paved the way for the final ousting of the corrupt officials.

Chapter Twelve

STRUGGLE WITHIN ISU BEGINS

In the meantime the rank and file seamen began to publish a mimeographed weekly known as the *ISU Pilot*. Its slogan was "Keep our union on a true course." In this weekly paper all of the anti-union practices of the officials were exposed. What took place at membership meetings was published in this paper and distributed by rank and filers on board the ships.

In retaliation the officials began the publication of a bulletin of their own. In this bulletin an open attack was made by the officials upon the foreign-born seamen. It was urged by the officials that the alien element was stopping the growth of the union. Actually, what the officials were doing was attempting to create that division between the alien and American seamen, the Negroes, the Filipinos, and the white seamen which would make unity almost impossible.

In the meantime, realizing the need for industrial unity, West Coast maritime workers were moving forward. At the close of the 1934 strike all of the West Coast maritime unions combined and formed the Maritime Federation of the Pacific. At a convention in Seattle, in April, 1935, Federation delegates unanimously adopted a resolution providing for a complete tie-up of all West Coast shipping unless demands for recognition were granted. A resolu-

tion was passed to proclaim July 5, Bloody Thursday, a
holiday to commemorate the death of two workers who
had been killed by the San Francisco police the previous
year. Another resolution adopted unanimously was a boycott against all Hearst publications because of their slan-
derous, lying, anti-union, strike-breaking statements.

The membership was soon to learn that only by organizing those who were still at that time unorganized and
building a strong ISU under the control of the membership would they be able to establish hiring through the
union hall. The rank and file members also began a fight
to reinstate two Pacific officials who had been expelled
from the union because they had been successful in
organizing a shipping committee.

LEGISLATIVE ATTACK

The next attack was in Congress. Bills had been introduced calling for a government hiring hall and for a continuous discharge book which would carry the photograph of all seamen and their fingerprints.

At a membership meeting of the East Coast MFOW
in May, 1935, Secretary Oscar Carlson openly approved
efforts being made in Washington to establish a government shipping hall. He said it would do away with the
crimps. He also stated that agitation for hiring through
the union hall was being carried on only in order to break
up the union. Membership meetings become more and
more distasteful to the officials of the union. Rank and
filers repeatedly demanded that hiring be done through
the union hall and that the officials oppose the anti-union
legislation which was then pending in Congress.

At several meetings Carlson attempted to clear the
union hall on the ground that it was unruly. On one

occasion he called the police who, upon learning that they were at a membership meeting in which regular business was being conducted, refused to clear the hall and stood by while the meeting was on.

In May, 1935, a rank and filer just off a ship wrote to the editor of the *ISU Pilot* asking how one went about getting shipping through the union hall. The answer was as follows:

In Port Arthur a motion was made to call a meeting of all seamen in port, organized and unorganized, to discuss this same question. This meeting was held and the seamen voted unanimously to ship only out of the union hall. So registration was begun with union members going to the top of the list, but all seamen registering thereafter went to the bottom of the list—union or non-union. This was not a violation of the constitution or the agreement because the shipowners still had the privilege of hiring their men where they pleased —*providing they could get them*—for the seamen refused to be hired outside of the union hall and enforced it by picketing all the crimps and shipping offices so the shipowners had to hire out of the union hall. Similar steps can be taken in the Port of New York and in other ports.

THE UNION ON THE SHIPS

In spite of the open opposition of the officials of the union, the ISU was being built on board the ships. The feeling generally was that if the ISU became strong, the rank and filers would be able to compel the officials to listen to them. A letter in the May 31 issue of the *ISU Pilot,* signed "Old Scrapper," is worth quoting in full because it illustrates the spirit of an honest-to-goodness rank and filer. It reads:

The other day I met an old shipmate of mine on the street,

and after usual greetings, the conversation, of course, turned into unionism, as usual. My friend showed me two union books, one ISU book and one scow captain's union book and told me that neither of them was any good—that he had stopped paying dues to either one of them.

I told him that that was not the way to make conditions better neither for himself nor anybody else, but that he could pay up his dues and help in the fight to make a good union.

He answered: That's impossible with that bunch of swivel chair warmers in office. They have been there so long that they practically own the "Damned Union."

Then I said: That's just it. We are fighting now to get them out of office, and elect officials from the rank and file.

Yes, he said: That's how the President of the United States is elected and for a little while after they get into office they are the best men in the world, but after half their time is up they are good to nobody but themselves.

By that time I had kind of warmed up so I told him hotly: No, the officials we (rank and file) elect, stays in office just exactly as long as the rank and file wants them to, and not a minute longer. And in case of a strike I said: We elect a strike committee, the best leaders, the best fighters, the best talkers, we can get hold of, boys who are not afraid of speaking out their minds to the shipowners. And not even *they* can sign any agreement with the shipowners, or make any arrangements until a meeting has been held and they have the consent of the majority of the rank and file.

He pondered on that a while, then he said: I guess you're right. I am going up and pay them right now. So we shook hands and parted.

AMENDMENT IGNORED

At a firemen's meeting in May, 1935, one of the members took the floor and proposed the following amendment to be included in the new constitution: "That all delegates be elected instead of being appointed by the officials." All were in favor of this except the patrolmen who spoke against it at length. Although the amendment was passed, it was not enforced.

Members of the National Maritime Union today would very likely be shocked to learn that a constitution could be written which permitted delegates to be appointed rather than elected. Yet the proposed firemen's constitution, which the officials were trying to ram down the throats of the rank and file seamen in 1935, actually provided for the appointment of delegates.

The demand, "all shipping through the union hall," was growing stronger every day among the members of the MFOW. The shipowners, however, refused to call the union for crews and their agents were seen running around looking for men in crimp joints and bar rooms. When membership meetings demanded that hiring take place through the union hall, the classical answer was that it was unconstitutional or that it was against the agreement, that everyone must have confidence in Oscar Carlson, one of the leaders, and that the shipowners wouldn't like it.

Naturally, the excuse that shipping through the union hall was against the agreement was but an attempt to confuse the seamen. There was nothing in the agreement which required seamen to walk the docks to secure jobs or to live in certain crimp joints in order to get a job. All that Article 2, Section 1, of the agreement said was:

It is understood and agreed that, as vacancies occur, members of the International Seamen's Union of America who are citizens of the United States shall be given preference of employment. . . .

But no one can say that Oscar Carlson was wrong when he said that "the shipowners won't like it." So much did the shipowners dislike it on the West Coast that it became necessary for the longshoremen to wage an eighty-one day strike for it. And on the East Coast the shipowners had been co-operating with the ISU officials to prevent hiring through the union hall.

"OLD-TIMER'S" LETTER

A letter published in the June 21, 1935, issue of the *ISU Pilot,* signed by an "old timer" from Hoboken, struck the keynote for the younger men who were then coming into the industry. It suggests the role that the old timer in a union can play in educating the newcomers into the union.

Some weeks ago I came across a copy of the *Pilot* over here in Hoboken and I read it with great interest. I could hardly believe my eyes when I got the more recent issues. I never thought I would see the day, and I have been going to sea for thirty years now, when we would have a rank and file committee in the ISU. I quit the union in 1921 because I could not stand for the loud speaker, Paddy Keane, and Gus Brown, the sea lawyer.

I have now rejoined the union, because I realize that with such a fine bunch of young American seamen* that was at the Sailors Union meeting two weeks ago, I know that I will see my hopes realized at a rank and file meeting. I heard sea bag Keane make his great speech, and it was the same old slumgullion, and I am now having faith again in having a union that will really fight for the average seamen.

* While it is true that there were many young people among the seamen, there were also many militants among its older seamen of native stock, and of various nationalities which was representative of the population of the United States.

Paddy Keane and Gus Brown think that they are the only Americans that are in America today, but some guy wrote once, that "patriotism is the last refuge of a scoundrel" and all the fakers can put that in their "kissers" and smoke it.

When I saw all the fine young Americans sitting there listening and smiling at his "crack pot shouting" about forty members, I know that the American Seaman is getting squared off to fight these fakers to the end.

I know there are many old timers like myself who will stick with you fellows to the end. Good Luck and a good fight. I would sign my name but I don't want the finger on me.

CARLSON'S NEXT MOVE

And a good fight it was that the young fellows, clasping the hands of the old timers, put up. Oscar Carlson, in order to rivet himself to his job in the MFOW, was about to put over his new constitution. It was the new spirit of old timers and newcomers in the MFOW that was responsible for his eventual defeat.

At the MFOW meeting of July 2, 1935, the balloting committee previously appointed by Mr. Carlson reported that altogether 134 members had voted. Imagine that kind of a vote on so important a matter as adopting a brand new constitution! According to the report, 119 men voted for it and 15 against it. Naturally, the report of this balloting committee was rejected by the membership. However, to put a stop to the enforcement of the new constitution, a group of rank and file seamen were compelled to institute court action to enjoin the enforcement of the constitution.

One provision of the constitution will give the seamen of today an idea of what the old line officials were attempting to do. Today NMU members have a constitution which provides that the pictures of prospective union officials be published in the union paper, that the ballots shall be secret and be counted by a disinterested Honest Balloting Association.

Section 7, Article XV, of the new MFOW constitution provided for the establishment of an Executive Board consisting of the trustees, chairman, secretary, and treasurer. The power that was vested in this Executive Board was as follows:

The Executive Board shall have a general supervision of all matters pertaining to the union and shall have *complete jurisdiction and power of disposition of all matters and questions referring as relating to the union or any of its members* or any branch of headquarters thereof, as well as of all matters and questions in which the said union headquarters, branches or members may be interested, or by which any of them may be in anywise affected. *The decision of the Executive Board shall be final.* (My italics—WLS.)

On August 14, five rank and file seamen instituted an action in the New York Supreme Court, demanding that a permanent injunction be issued against enforcement of a new MFOW constitution, on the ground that it was adopted in violation of the existing constitution. The ultimate trial for the injunction did not take place until the spring of 1936, right in the midst of the spring strike.

While the courts finally decided against the seamen, the court fight served as a rallying point for the rank and file in their fight for union democracy. The most important result of the court action was not the final court decision but the tremendous strengthening of the organized rank and file movement in the ISU.

The power vested by this new constitution in the Executive Board is surpassed in arrogance only by the

constitution which David E. Grange, president of the
Cooks and Stewards Union, "declared" in effect on January 31, 1935, at the same time that the agreement signed
with the shipowners went into effect. Under the Cooks
and Stewards constitution, Grange, once having been
elected, held "office until two-thirds of the entire membership decided by referendum vote that his services are
no longer required." His powers included the right "to
suspend any officer of the Union from active duty until
such time as the Executive Board shall give its final decision regarding any complaint pending against the suspended officers. . . ." And since the MCS constitution
made no provision for the holding of a referendum vote,
David E. Grange would have been able to remain in
office and receive his $10,000 a year salary for the rest of
his life.

Chapter Thirteen

EVENTS LEADING TO SPRING STRIKE

As early as October, 1935, the rank and file seamen
were discussing renewal of the agreement expiring on
December 31. The union had grown from a shell of a
little more than a thousand to approximately 14,000.

In the meantime, ISU officials issued their call for the

thirty-third national convention, scheduled to open in Washington, January 31, 1936. The Boston membership immediately got busy and elected two rank and filers— Moe Byne and Jack Montal—to represent them at this convention.

Ships' crews adopted sharp resolutions and sent them in to headquarters. The *SS California* was among the first. It demanded:

1. All shipping be done through the union hall.
2. Overtime pay for all overtime work.
3. The right to strike if the agreement is violated by the shipowners.
4. In case of a ship entering a strike area the crew will not handle cargo, will not supply steam and will not pass through a picket line.

The resolution concluded: That the Atlantic district of the ISU as a step toward national unity of the three districts shall strive for a national agreement and a national scale of wages.

At membership meetings, officials reported that the negotiating committee was going to ask for a 25 per cent increase in wages and 75 cents an hour overtime. Nothing was said about shipping through the union hall. The rank and file demanded that this provision be incorporated into the new agreement. More important, they demanded that the agreement be submitted to a general vote before it be considered in effect. The demand that regular meetings be held was also repeatedly raised at meetings and urged through the pages of the *ISU Pilot*.

FINK HALL PROPOSED

As the time for renewing the agreement approached, officials of the union proposed the following: "A centralized shipping bureau managed co-jointly by the same shipowners and the unions affiliated with the International Seamen's Union of America."

Shipping through the union hall strengthened the Longshoremen's Union as well as the maritime unions on the West Coast. The shipowners knew that as long as they could maintain their own hiring halls and their own crimp halls they could also maintain their own blacklist and their own group of "loyal" company men—finks—to man their ships in time of a struggle.

The seamen, on the other hand, knew that union hiring meant doing away with discrimination and blacklisting. It meant doing away with "letter" boys, with rich men's sons making trips "for the fun of it." It meant that as long as there were jobs available, they would be given to all seamen on a rotary basis.

On December 21, 1935, the seamen read in the newspapers that the shipowners had refused to consider demands presented by the Negotiating Committee. The demands were for a 25 per cent increase in wages, 75 cents an hour for overtime pay, increased crews and jointly controlled hiring halls. The shipowners refused point-blank to grant any concessions. All they would offer was to renew the old agreement for another year.

Discussion of the new agreement became heated. Resolutions were being introduced to prepare for the fight, felt to be inevitable. Some crews were even beginning to talk with their feet. The crew of the SS Pennsylvania struck on January 4, 1936, while the vessel was lying in the port of San Francisco, demanding that West Coast articles and West Coast pay be met.

The crew was asked to bring the ship back to New York on a promise that upon its arrival their grievances would be taken up. When the ship arrived, not only was the promise not kept, but all the leaders of the crew were fired and blacklisted. The treatment of the crew of the *SS Pennsylvania* by the United States Lines was the spark which ultimately set the crew of the *SS California* into motion and lead to the spring strike.

On January 10, ballots were being prepared for a referendum vote on the question of the renewal of the 1935 agreement. The ballots were to read: "As you in favor of extending the present agreement until January 1, 1937?"

ISU CONVENTION

In the meantime, the ISU convention had opened in Washington. Moe Byne and Jack Montal, elected by the Boston branch of the MFOW to go to the convention as "observers," received a great deal of support from the West Coast delegates but were prevented from being seated. Ship crews, in the meantime, were deluging the convention with letters and postcards urging a uniform national agreement. Crews were urging that the ISU establish a National Maritime Federation and that a national uniform agreement be adopted under which East Coast and West Coast seamen would enjoy the same conditions. But the convention was under the complete domination of the East Coast officials and the national officers. The convention voted to open a broad attack on the Maritime Federation of the Pacific.

The Sailors Union of the Pacific had its charter lifted by a handful of East Coast officials and its 13,000 members suddenly found themselves outside the ISU. The reason: The SUP had supported the Federation and had refused to reinstate Paul Scharrenburg, SUP secretary, who had been expelled by a general referendum vote.

A delegation of East Coast seamen appeared before the convention and presented the following petition to the delegates:

We seamen of New York, feeling that our sentiments on these questions should be made known to the convention, authorize the following petition to be presented:

We are opposed to the convention ordering the reorganization of the West Coast unions and forcing them to withdraw from the Maritime Federation. We want unity with the West Coast; we want democracy in the East and Gulf, in order that we can win the same kind of wages and working conditions as those prevailing on the West Coast.

This was ignored by the convention.

The convention also adopted a resolution favoring shipping board control of hiring and favoring the continuous service discharge book, the "fink" book. This book, you will recall, carried a seaman's photograph, his fingerprints and a record of his work, that is, whether it was "good" or "bad." This proved an excellent device because, naturally, the work of a seaman with union sympathies seldom was characterized by anti-union masters as "good."

RENEWAL REJECTED

During the month of January a referendum vote of the membership was conducted, from Boston to Port Arthur, to determine whether or not the 1935 agreement should be renewed. When the results came out, the position of the rank and file was made clear. Out of 7,826 union members who voted in the referendum, 5,897 voted against renewal and only 1,929 voted in favor of renewal. A statement was signed by the balloting committee making the following recommendations:

In our opinion the referendum just held on the question of renewal of the old agreement has given a fair expression to the sentiment of the union membership and while there are many members who have not voted, the vote cast is a good indication of the consensus of opinion of the entire membership.

Therefore we think that the unions notify the shipowners that we are ready to reopen negotiations for a better agreement. It is the unanimous opinion of the balloting committee that the union should get a deadline by which time shipowners should grant a better agreement.

This statement was read at a sailors' union meeting in New York on February 17, 1936.

Evidence that ISU officials were working against the interests of the membership during these days is a letter written in longhand February 23, 1936, by Victor Olander, national secretary of the ISU, to Grange, Carlson and Brown. This letter, which came into the possession of a rank and filer and was later published in the New York newspapers, reveals clearly the corruption of which these men were capable. The letter reads:

I was told over the telephone this morning that some of the agitators are talking of attempting strikes along the waterfront here in New York within the next week or so. I have no means of knowing whether or not there is anything to the story beyond mere talk.

The thought occurs to me however that the claim may be made that the proposals to renew the agreement having been rejected by referendum vote, there is now no agreement at all and that therefore all hands are free to strike at will.

To offset any such move, I believe it would be wise to

report to the Unions and to *announce publicly* that negotiations have been reopened, that the first meeting has been held, that another will follow probably some time this week and that it has been agreed by both the Seamen's Committee and the Shipowners Committee that the 1935 agreement will continue in full force and effect while the negotiations are going on.

Obviously no such negotiations were in progress and Olander was simply suggesting that the officials issue a fraudulent public statement. Although negotiations were extended for thirty days, no action was being taken by East Coast officials to prepare for a strike if the shipowners persisted in their demands that the old 1935 agreement be renewed.

Ivan Hunter, vice-president of the ISU, shortly after the 1936 Convention left for the West Coast where he undertook the organization of a new and dual union to be known as the "ISU, Sailors Division, Pacific Coast District." The shipowners, very likely by pre-arrangement, endorsed this new union. Hugh Gallagher, president of the Pacific Shipowners Association, stated:

The Pacific Shipowners have no desire to become involved in any jurisdictional controversy in the union. However, our contracts and our arbitration award are with the Seamen's Union. Therefore shipowners have no alternative but to continue to deal with the *legally constituted* representatives of the ISU. (My italics—W.L.S.)

SS *CALIFORNIA* INCIDENT

On Monday, March 1, 1936, the entire crew of the *SS California* struck in San Pedro demanding the West Coast scale of wages. The shipowners were forced to admit in this case that the crews struck because they wanted better wages and conditions and not because of "intimidation by Pacific Coast Union men ashore."

Secretary of Labor Frances Perkins, who was attending a Cabinet dinner given by President Roosevelt, left the dinner table to speak to Joseph Curran, the representative of the crew of the *SS California,* by phone. In a press conference, March 5, she said:

I asked the men to go back to work, and they held a meeting in the back of the butcher shop. I held the wire, talking the while to Mr. Fitzgerald, our conciliator.

It was about half an hour before the meeting was over, and the committee decided to recommend that the crew man the ship and continue the trip to New York. . . .

I pledged the men that I would see to it that their point of view was laid before the negotiating committee. I also pledged them that I would use my best offices to see to it that there would be no discrimination against them as to future employment.

On March 9, while the *California* was on its way back to the East Coast, the ISU officials signed a new agreement which provided a $5 wage increase with no concessions for overtime pay or any provision for hiring through the union hall. Even the proposal of union officials that a joint hiring hall be established was rejected. This agreement, which was to run for two years, was nothing but a renewal of the 1935 agreement with the exception of the $5 increase, and was not submitted to a referendum.

It was the hope of the shipowners and the officials that within these two years they would be able, through the power vested in them by the new Constitutions, not only completely to eliminate the rank and file from their deliberations but also to smash the Maritime Federation of the Pacific.

In the meantime, Secretary of Commerce Daniel Roper was demanding that the crew of the SS *California* be prosecuted as mutineers, overriding the suggestions of Secretary Perkins. Trotting out the old cry that safety of life at sea would be seriously jeopardized if discipline were not rigidly maintained, Roper suggested that the Department of Justice take direct action.

"MUTINEERS" BLACKLISTED

Upon the return of the SS *California* to New York, sixty-four crew members were fired and blacklisted. The crew declared the ship on strike and a few days later issued the following statement to all members of the ISU:

The *California* crew is on strike. The *American Trader* has followed our example. We are fighting for a better union agreement and to prevent ISU members from being fired, fined and blacklisted.

Instead of coming to the support of our strike, the District Committee has issued a strike-breaking leaflet stating that "there is no strike on the *California* or any other ships of the IMM lines" and that "IMM lines are signatories to the agreement with the ISU."

We are striking for the following reasons:

After three months of negotiations between a self-appointed negotiations committee and the shipowners, a new agreement was finally reached with about 30 shipping companies.

The membership has never voted upon or otherwise approved of any agreement reached by the district committee with the shipowners.

While this agreement gives the seaman a $5 wage increase, it does not provide for overtime pay or union control of hiring, and would shackle us to these conditions for two years.

At last Monday night's sailors meeting, the membership went on record against any agreement which did not provide for overtime pay or which ran for two years. We want an agreement that expires the same time as the West Coast.

The membership also demanded that immediate action be taken in the negotiations and this action be backed up with strike action to force every steamship company to sign a satisfactory agreement.

Three members of the Executive Board at Monday's meeting denied that they knew anything about the proposed agreement being endorsed by the Executive Board—*and certainly it has not been voted upon by the membership.*

Promises were made to the crew of the California by such high officers as Secretary of Labor Perkins that no member of the crew would be discriminated against because of his union activities and the strike action in San Pedro. But, on arrival in New York, 64 men were fired, blackballed and many were logged.

Our union officials and the government labor representatives have by these actions aided the shipowners.

Are we going to see union men fired and logged because of their union activities? Are we going to be shackled to an agreement which does not give us overtime pay and union control of hiring?

In striking the *California* and *American Trader* we are taking the only course left to us, to every other loyal member, *and every other ship's crew,* to get overtime pay for all work over eight hours and to abolish the blacklist and crimps. The shipowners with the aid of the officials have refused to settle these burning grievances after months of negotiations.

Therefore, we call upon other ships' crews in this port and every other port: *Follow the example of the crew of the* "California" *and the* "Trader"!

The ISU belongs to the membership. The West Coast seamen have shown us how to gain better conditions and how to rid the union of traitors. Let's follow their example.

Support the crews of the "California" and the "Trader!"
Protest the leaflet of the District Committee! Demand that
the strike on the "California" and the "Trader" be officially
recognized, endorsed and supported.
These are our and your demands:

1. West Coast scale of wages.
2. 75 cents an hour overtime.
3. Shipping through the union hall.
4. Eight hour day for stewards.
5. Agreement to expire same time as West Coast, September 30.

Strike for These Demands on Every Ship—Everybody
on the Picket Line!

(Signed)

Joe Curran, 5499   P. Codyre, 5509
R. Manning, 7636   J. S. Paine, 4170
B. Meers, 4419   T. Murray, 3514

This call was answered by dozens of ships' crews who, as soon as their ships docked and they were told what was happening, left their ships and joined the picket line. A strike committee was established by the strikers and plans were made to strike all ships and enlist public support.

Chapter Fourteen

SPRING STRIKE, 1936

Attempts were made to force the ISU officials to en-
dorse the strike, but, of course, with very little success.
All the time the strike was going on, the strike committee
and Joseph Curran, chairman, made it quite clear that
this was a fight of the rank and file. The committee said:

*Don't let anyone get the idea that we are breaking away
from the union. That's out. It is our union. We built it.
Not the Carlsons or Browns. It belongs to the waterfront.
We are keeping it there. We speak for 35,000 seamen and
not for eleven men.*

The press began an open attack upon the strike referring to it constantly as an outlaw strike. The Hearst
papers charged that the strike must be laid to reds. The
mayor was being petitioned by the Hearst papers "to
give strong policing in the outlaw strike."

On the other hand, the West Coast shipowners were
whipping up their campaign against Harry Bridges and
the Maritime Federation of the Pacific. Presidents of
steamship companies issued such statements as the following:

. . . Bridges and the left-wing elements in control of the
Seamen's Union have done their best to discourage continu-

ous employment by refusing to let men make more than a voyage or two on the same vessel.

Charges that seamen were attempting to take control of all shipping through a National Maritime Federation were released to the public. One shipowner stated:

. . . Once having secured that control, the next step will be control of all trucks by refusing to handle cargoes to or from truck owners who do not submit to affiliation with the Maritime Federation. If that move is successful, the next step is to secure control of the railroad unions. Once that is secured, Bridges and his group will control the distribution of the country and whoever controls distribution rules the country. This may seem extravagant and farfetched, yet we shipowners on the Pacific Coast in the light of what has happened do not think that Bridges' goal is impossible of attainment.

One newspaper story carried this headline: "Strikers viewed as Red Puppets by Conservatives in the Ships Union." There were many others of the same tenor. The officials of the East Coast unions whose conduct precipitated the strike were quoted as authorities that the striking seamen were as a matter of fact reds and not Americans at all.

HITS RED SCARE

The strikers, on the other hand, made it quite clear that all they wanted was human treatment. Joseph Curran, in an interview with newspapermen, pointed out that all the men were asking was (1) that hiring take place through a central hiring hall, and (2) that seamen have something to say about their own working and living conditions on board ship. On the red scare, Curran said:

Some people are trying to drag us into politics, but we don't know anything about politics. We're just sailors. We know that anybody who goes out and tries to get better wages and conditions will be called Reds and radicals. If that's being radical, we're radical.

We're not trying to tear down the American Constitution, American institutions or the American Merchant Marine. On the contrary, we're trying to build them up. Give us a square deal and the men would be so well satisfied that we would have the finest merchant marine in the world, and there wouldn't be any more talk about communism.

By May 6, forty-five ships' crews were striking and a port-wide strike was declared. A mass picket line was organized around the striking piers. At first, attempts were made to interfere with the right of mass picketing, but that failed.

STRIKE-BREAKING ATTEMPTS

Although the spring strike turned out to be a curtain-raiser for the more intensive and more trying fall strike a few months later, it was no Sunday picnic.

After the *California* crew struck, a little time was required for the ships' crews coming into the port to become aware of what actually happened. And as they piled off the ships, they found the shipowners engaged in a frenzied effort to replace them. ISU officials kept referring to the strike as an "outlaw" strike and gave direct aid to the shipowners.

The shipowners insisted that the strikers had breached an agreement. It was not possible for the striking seamen, with the limited sources at their command, to make the public understand that the agreement hurriedly renewed on March 9 was the one which had been rejected in the

January referendum. A little more than a month prior to this hurried renewal of the 1935 agreement, the seamen had rejected the proposed renewal by a referendum. The claim, therefore, that the spring strike, or for that matter the fall strike, was illegal is unfounded.

Officials of the International Longshoremen's Association joined with the shipowners and the ISU officials in their campaign to recruit crews for the tied-up ships. The city of Cleveland and the city of Boston were established as central points for the gathering of strikebreakers. Yorkville, a German-American neighborhood in New York City, already a flourishing hotbed of Nazis, was the concentration point for scabs. Striking seamen were successful in persuading many crews not to sail. Some ships, however, moved.

STRIKE ENDED

As a result of the effectiveness of the strike, the International Executive Board of the ISU was compelled to offer the seamen the following terms in order to terminate the strike. The Executive Committee had pledged to help prevent any blacklisting to secure a square deal for those members who had been arbitrarily "expelled for participating in the strike" and to see to it that mediation and conciliation boards were set up to adjust the grievances and demands raised by the strikers.

At a mass meeting of striking seamen in New York on May 28, a proposal was made and adopted to accept the settlement terms proposed by the ISU Executive Board to terminate the strike.

The Joint Strike Committee stated:

Our fight for a powerful union and for decent conditions

on the ships has just begun. We have dealt a powerful blow
to our enemies both within and without our ranks. The
strike showed that our strength is growing and we came out
of the strike stronger than ever.

On with the fight! Forward to a powerful rank and file
controlled International Seamen's Union and a Maritime
Federation in the East and Gulf.

That the cause of the seamen impressed itself upon
the community at large is borne out by a list of contributions to the strike fund. Here we see that persons from
every walk of life recognized the justness of the cause of
the striking seamen and were willing to support it
financially.

Seven professors from the Columbia University faculty
sent in their contributions. The following also con-
tributed: Brooklyn College students; the Models Union;
Greek Workers Educational Club; Musicians Group;
Fish Workers Union; Socialist Party, Chelsea Branch;
Painters Union; Provincetown Playhouse; Norwegian
Workers; American Musicians Alliance; Artists Union;
Waterfront Section, Communist Party; Cafeteria Workers
Union; Utica Workers Club; N. Y. U. Students; Ameri-
can League Against War and Fascism; Followers of
Nature; Upper Harlem Women's Club; Newspaper
Guild; Estonian and Latvian Youth Club; Furriers Joint
Council of New York; Progressive Women's Council;
Allentown Workers Club; Jewish Writers' Union; Dress-
makers' Union; Independent Houseworkers' Union;
Communist Party, Queens County; Young Workers'
Athletic Club; City Committee for Striking Seamen;
Anti-War Youth League; Civic Repertory Theater; and
Painters' Local 174.

When the strike ended, the rank and file seamen elected

a Seamen's Defense Committee. This committee was to remain ashore to protect the interests of the rank and file seamen, as well as to do all in their power to bring about the release of a group of strikers who had been imprisoned during the strike.

Chapter Fifteen

ISU OFFICIALS IN THE COURTS

During the months immediately following the strike, Congress enacted a bill providing for the continuous discharge book. For more than a year, the fight against this book preoccupied not only the Seamen's Defense Committee but the Strike Strategy Committee—a committee elected in the fall of the year to conduct the final struggle that was ultimately to rid the seamen of their parasitic leadership.

In the meantime, a group of rank and file seamen in the Cooks and Stewards Union decided to institute legal action against David E. Grange, president of the union. As we saw earlier, Grange had such complete control of his union that the rank and file had no say whatever in its affairs. Under his "amended" constitution, he was in office by almost appointing himself to it. Meetings were held but once a month, which made it difficult for the membership to express their views as effectively as in the MFOW or the Sailors Union, both of which had more frequent meetings.

So clearly was Grange working with the International Mercantile Marine that in the very midst of the spring strike, on May 20, he felt obliged to submit the script of a radio address to a vice president of the IMM, who made the following comment: "I think it is a very excellent statement and hope it will have the effect of nullifying the talk given by non-union seaman Curran."

The rank and file seamen sought to compel Grange to account for the vast sums of money which had came into the union with the increase in the number of initiation fees and dues paid by a vast number of new members who had joined the union since the unions were reorganized.

ACCOUNTING DEMANDED

In the court action, Grange was asked to explain the disappearance of $144,358 in union funds. In the seventeen months between January 1, 1935, and June 1, 1936, the union's income was $238,861 in dues and initiation fees. After deducting the legitimate expenses of the union $144,000 should have been left.

Grange had publicly stated that he withdrew $30,000 to reimburse himself for money advanced as strike expenses. In an affidavit, Octave Loones, a delegate in the employ of the Marine Cooks and Stewards Union, said that although he attended almost every meeting of the union since 1935, he had never heard Grange refer to any strike in which members of the union were involved, much less one which might cost the union $30,000.

Other affidavits of former union officials alleged that Grange had been receiving subsidies from union officials. Henry P. Griffin, president of the MCS union between

1903 and 1921, said that Grange, before he succeeded to the presidency of the MCS, was employed as a delegate and "collector," and in the latter capacity he collected, prior to 1922, the following monthly subsidies from steamship companies:

Eastern Steamship Company	$200
United Fruit Company	200
Savannah Line	100
Clyde Mallory Line	200
Morgan Line	200
Ward Line	200
Porto Rican Line	100

In all, a total of $1,200 per month. These revelations explained in part the disastrous strike conducted by the ISU in 1921. The receipt of subsidies from steamship companies was by no means an original idea with Grange. The Griffin affidavit also charged that similar payments were made by lines to Gus Brown and Oscar Carlson, both of whom were still active officials of their unions.

MFOW ELECTIONS

While Grange was being exposed, an election of officers was conducted under the new constitution of the MFOW. The rank and file slate headed by Frederick C. Phillips and Moe Byne, running for secretary and treasurer respectively, was elected by a two to one majority. Carlson, for the first time in many years, was out of office. The progressive slate contained a few of the old line officials, those who were believed to be free from the contamination of the top officials and whom the rank and file believed they could trust.

When the newly elected officials, however, came into the union hall to demand that Carlson turn over to them the books and whatever money remained in the treasury, he refused. He was arrested and immediately, with Ernest Misland, applied to the court for an injunction to restrain Phillips and Byne from performing their duties. This injunction was denied.

The International secretary Ivan Hunter was then called in. He, too, instituted an action—this time in the Federal Court—demanding that new MFOW officers be restrained from fulfilling their duties.

Meanwhile, the shipowners were co-operating with the old-line officials by refusing to issue passes to permit newly elected delegates of the MFOW to visit the ships.

Rank and file indignation rose and a sitdown strike took place on several ships, including the SS Roosevelt.

During the Federal Court fight instituted by the ISU officers, rank and file seamen were interested only in one thing: Would the shipowners recognize their duly elected officials? If not, they would remain on strike. The Federal judge who heard Hunter's application recommended that all parties enter into an agreement to be signed in his presence, permitting him to designate an arbitrator who would supervise a new election.

So convinced were the rank and file seamen of the justness of their cause that, even though they had insisted that the rank and file election conducted under the new constitution was a valid one, they signed the stipulation. An arbitrator was appointed and the ships sailed immediately. Under the stipulation, Ivan Hunter agreed to have two sets of passes issued to enable not only the rank and file officials to board the ships but the old officials in office prior to the election of the new slate. This agreement was never lived up to, but the coming of the fall strike resolved the issue.

Chapter Sixteen

EVENTS LEADING TO FALL STRIKE

While strike action was begun by the crew of the *SS Roosevelt* and other vessels on the East Coast, negotiations were in progress on the West Coast for the renewal of the West Coast agreements of the longshoremen and maritime unions expiring on September 30. The shipowners on the West Coast were in their own way trying to force a coast strike in an attempt to smash the union.

In anticipation of the negotiations, the West Coast operators had been engaged in sensational newspaper stories and radio broadcasts for almost a year. During the months immediately preceding the negotiations and while negotiations were on, this campaign was supplemented by paid advertisements.

The West Coast unions remembering the unrestrained provocation of the shipowners during the 1934 strike, submitted a full statement of the facts to the public during the month of September.

It was clear that the Pacific Coast shipowners were preparing for a showdown. The possibility of another struggle, similar to the 1934 one, was discussed in the press. The maritime unions pointed out the fascist program of the shipowners. All the operators were interested in, they said, was the re-establishment of the deplorable conditions that existed prior to the 1934 maritime strike.

While the arbiter's award to the longshoremen which followed the 1934 strike gave them substantial gains, this was not true in the case of the seagoing maritime unions. You will recall that on December 6, 1934, long before any award was handed down affecting the rights of the seagoing maritime unions, an agreement was entered into between the old line ISU officials and the shipowners under which seamen were still to receive $60 a month and not to be paid for overtime. Living quarters still remained uninhabitable, with as many as eight and ten men sleeping in one room.

ILWU CONDITIONS

The longshoremen, on the other hand, had in a measure removed the evil of blacklisting and discrimination through the establishment of centralized hiring through union halls. They were now dispatched in a prompt and business-like manner to the place where they were needed. They were no longer required to hang around waterfront saloons waiting for a chance to "treat" the hiring bosses. They did not have to fawn or lick anyone's boots to get a job. Neither did they have to worry lest the next fellow was going to get ahead of them. In short, they could afford the luxury of being men.

Another important change had taken place between 1934 and 1936. In an article published in the middle of September, Harry Bridges said:

Today *there are no unemployed longshoremen.* All are working and the work is evenly distributed. There are no "preferred gangs" working to the point of exhaustion. And there are *no longshoremen on relief.* Through the collective action of the men, themselves, the burden of their support has been removed from the backs of the taxpayers and is placed squarely where it belongs—upon the shipping industry.

Nevertheless, the shipowners on the West Coast were preparing for a showdown. As a matter of fact this was true of shipowners on the East Coast as well. The Maritime Federation of the Pacific Coast was strong. The unity between the longshoremen and the maritime unions was firm and the shipowners were girding themselves for a final fight.

Why did they want a showdown? Was it because business was bad and increased wages would become a severe drain upon their profits? By no means! Business was good. Profits were soaring. For example; between 1920 and 1927 the net income of the Matson Navigation Company had risen from $1,245,248 to $2,375,826. Wages of engineers, on the other hand, had dropped from $200 a month to $165. In 1932, the worst year of the depression, the Matson Company showed a net income of $1,397,929, or $152,645 above the 1920 figure. Engineers' wages had dropped to $140 per month. In 1934, the company's net income rose to $2,962,305, the highest figure in the company's history. But engineers' wages had dropped again to $130 per month. From 1920 to 1934, the net worth of the Matson Navigation Company had increased 234 per cent. Meanwhile, it had paid $14,593,495 in cash dividends and $27,711,700 in stock dividends. Certainly the depression had not hit this company very hard. Other shipping companies did almost as well.

They wanted a showdown because they hoped to

smash union organization. In a report to President Roosevelt, Postmaster General James A. Farley estimated the amount of the government subsidies that were being paid in the form of mail contracts, sale of ships, and low interest rates on construction loans as $708,618,096.06. Salaries paid to a Dollar Steamship Company official between 1923 and 1932, inclusive, amounted to more than $14,000,000. While the salary and bonuses of R. S. Dollar during that period rose 281.4 per cent, the wages of the engineers on the Dollar Line showed no change at all between 1923 and 1931.

Therefore, the showdown that was being planned in the fall of 1936 could not be attributed to the high wages of workers. What, then, was the reason? To quote one of the West Coast union officials:

> The real secret of their present inflamed state of mind can be put in one word—*control*. For 14 years they had full control of the waterfront. By a system of blacklisting and discrimination, they were able to starve or frighten the waterfront workers into submission. They have the old predatory "overlord's" attitude toward industrial relations. They want to deal with "dependents," grateful for handouts—not with *men*. They cannot—or will not—adjust themselves to the New Era that has come to the waterfront. Still in their eyes, they are the *masters,* we are the *slaves.*

SHIPOWNERS ARM

In the meantime the West Coast shipowners were beginning to arm for a virtual war on the maritime unions. They were backed by Hearst, the Liberty League, and the Republican Party, all of whom wanted to embarrass the Roosevelt administration before the 1936 election.

The *Commonwealth News* of Seattle revealed that the

Law and Order League, the open shop organization of waterfront employers in Seattle, had hired three hundred gunmen and were distributing large quantities of guns and ammunition. A reporter of the *News,* posing as an applicant for a job as a guard, drew the following statement from "Tanker" Smith, a notorious killer and gunman recruiter:

> When the mobs start coming out here on the waterfront, I want you to shoot—and shoot to kill. . . . There's 30 million dollars' worth of shipping companies and 90 million dollars' worth of oil companies backing you when you kill anybody here.

The close but secret link between the strike-provoking shipowners and the Republicans was revealed in a note from Smith vouching for the reporter in his role of gunman job-seeker: "Matt: O.K. for guard duty by Ralph Horr." Horr, a prominent attorney, was the Republican candidate for the gubernatorial nomination in the primaries.

As September drew to a close, the shipowners threatened a lockout, but it was averted by an extension of the negotiations for fifteen days. Later the Maritime Commission ordered the truce extended for another fifteen days. The union leaders on the West Coast stood flatly against the arbitration of certain points, such as the retention of the union hiring halls and a guarantee of the right to refrain from passing through or working behind picket lines. The shipowners were demanding blind arbitration as a substitute for negotiations. It was made clear by the West Coast seamen that the eight-hour day with overtime provision and the union hiring hall were two fundamental principles that could not be arbitrated. They felt that it would be like asking the American public to arbitrate religion or slavery. Seeking arbitration on such issues meant only one thing—an effort to break the unions.

WEST COAST STRIKE BEGINS

On October 30, 1936, Joseph Curran, chairman of the Seamen's Defense Committee, arrived in San Francisco. His role at the West Coast, as indicated at the time of his arrival, was that of an observer for the East Coast seamen. The Joint Negotiations Committee of the maritime unions blasted all rumors that a "split had occurred in the unions over the issue of polling a strike vote." At a meeting of the Sailors Union of the Pacific, it was declared that the scheduled strike vote would go through as planned. When, on October 30, the owners refused to negotiate any further, the strike began. Over three hundred ships were struck on the West Coast.

Joseph Curran returned to New York with the proposal that the East Coast seamen give their full support to the West Coast strike and that they organize a strike to secure an adequate agreement for themselves.

In spite of all efforts by the ISU officials to prevent action, crews on ships in New York and other East Coast ports began going off their ships. In an attempt to stem the rising tide, the union officials called a mass meeting at Cooper Union on November 4th, in New York, to persuade the men not to strike. Fifteen hundred seamen came to this meeting.

Joseph Curran and the other members of the Seamen's Defense Committee were barred from the meeting. For several hours, the ISU officials tried all the tricks of the trade to discourage the men, but to no avail.

Police were brought into the meeting and attempts were made to break it up. These also failed. Finally, the rank and file opened the doors and brought Curran and his committee to the platform to conduct the meeting. The feeling of the seamen at this meeting can be judged by the following exchange:

Curran: In a press release in which John M. Franklin, president of IMM, makes certain charges, Franklin states that you have an agreement lasting until the end of the year 1937. As you are all members of the ISU, did any of you get a chance to vote on the ratification of this agreement?

Answer from the membership: No!!! Unanimous.

Curran: Were any of the members of your families ever threatened while you were away at sea?

Emphatic answer from the entire body present: No.

Curran: Were any of you men ever forced or intimidated to pay tribute for "clearance cards" by anyone on or connected with the waterfront?

ISU membership: No! (many boos for Franklin.)

Curran: Do you know of any gangsters being connected with the Strike Committee?

Membership in a unanimous voice: No!!!

Curran: Do you know these seamen who are on the Strike Committee?

Answer from membership: Yes!!!

Curran: Do you know of any members of the Strike Committee who are not legitimate seamen or who have never been at sea?

Membership, loudly: No!!!

Brother Curran then asked if there was anyone in the audience who was coerced in any way to come out on strike, that this is a democratic meeting and everyone has a right to state what is in his mind whether he agrees with us or not.

There was no answer from the audience and it was very plain to everyone including the press who were present that all those members present had come off the ships of their own free will in support of their West Coast brothers.

The membership voted to call a general coastwise conference where the question of a coastwise strike was to be decided.

Chapter Seventeen

FALL STRIKE, 1936

After the Cooper Union meeting, a mass meeting was called by the Seamen's Defense Committee which declared that the East Coast seamen were on strike.

In addition to pledging full support to the West Coast strikers, the East Coast seamen raised their own demands which were as follows:

1. West Coast wages and conditions.
2. Sixty cents per hour—cash payment for all overtime.
3. Union hiring halls.
4. Eight hours for the Stewards Department.

This meeting also elected a strike strategy committee composed of the following: Joseph Curran, Ferdinand C. Smith, Al Lannon, Blackie Keenan, Glen Skogman, John Muldarig, Charles McCarthy, and Frank Jones.

The spirit of the striking men was that of crusaders. Crew after crew piled off. Scabherders were retained by the shipowners and the ISU officials were giving whatever help they could to place scabs on ships. The famous strikebreaker, Sam "Chowderhead" Cohen, was visited by six strikers at his ritzy room at the Hotel Claridge and he agreed not to meddle in the strike. The seamen, however, called the police and both Cohen and one of his men were removed to a police station for investigation by the FBI. Grange, too, was arrested on a charge of felonious assault. He was charged with attacking a seaman and brandishing a gun in his face.

ISU officials attempted to obtain an injunction against the strikers in Philadelphia, but failed.

In the meantime, Ivan Hunter, who had half-heartedly signed the agreement for an election in the MFOW under the court's supervision, notified the Judge, Murray Hulbert, that because of the strike situation, he could no longer accede to the terms of that stipulation. On November 25, Judge Hulbert, who had earnestly hoped to resolve the dispute within this union, finally denied the injunction which Carlson sought to obtain against the newly elected officials. Frederick Phillips and Moe Byne were, in effect, declared to be the duly elected officials of the MFOW.

SCABHERDING

Scabherding grew. The winter cold was beginning to be felt by the thinly-clad and poorly-fed strikers. Shipowners tactics were to concentrate on the East Coast strike. The West Coast was comparatively quiet. At tremendous cost, the shipowners were trying their utmost to sail their ships in the Atlantic and Gulf in order to break what they considered the strike's weakest link. The IMM had been hardest hit; every one of its Panama

Pacific Line ships were still tied up to the docks during the first weeks in December.

The shipping commissioner for the port of New York had threatened publicly to "sail ships at all costs." Rumors were circulated that the licensed officers were going to withdraw from the strike, but all along the Atlantic and Gulf coasts, members of the Masters, Mates and Pilots and the Marine Engineers Beneficial Association repudiated these unfounded rumors. Charges were brought against the commissioner of the port of New York because of his utter disregard of the safety-at-sea laws in permitting vessels to leave the port of New York completely undermanned. Letters were written to President Roosevelt and Secretary of Commerce Roper protesting against government officials aiding and abetting the shipowners by violating safety laws.

On December 17, Harry Bridges and Joseph Curran addressed a vast meeting at Madison Square Garden. They told of working conditions on the East Coast. They said that if the maritime workers were to be restored to the status of civilized beings, conditions then prevailing on board ships would have to be remedied. Gloryholes on passenger vessels were known to accommodate as many as twenty and sometimes thirty stewards, with no accommodations made for storing their simplest belongings.

TRIBUTE TO KANE

At this meeting, tribute was also paid to Johnnie Kane who had been shot in cold blood by a notorious goon-squad organizer, Wilbur Dickey, in Houston, Texas. Kane died Tuesday, December 16, the day before the mass meeting.

In the meantime, some of the vessels were sailing. The Grace Liner *Santa Elena* left with a scab and inefficient crew, piled up on the rocks in Cartagena, Columbia.

The strikers had other enemies besides guns, gunmen, and scabherders. The winter season was beginning to take its toll. On a trip along the East Coast that winter, the writer visited several union halls. At Philadelphia, late one evening, a group of strikers were huddled together in a bare loft building, one end of which was kept warm by a small coal stove. Some of the seamen were sleeping on the floor around the stove, with nothing but newspaper for bedding and covers. A few who were about to go on watch were washing and tending to their feet. Their spirit never failed but some came down with pneumonia as a result of exposure on the picket lines.

The shipowners missed no tricks in their efforts to break the strike. One of their representatives even wormed his way into the councils of the Strike Strategy Committee. After three months of strike, rumors that seamen were returning to the ships, that the strike was being lost, began to circulate, apparently by persons interested in sabotaging the strike. Where these rumors emanated from was difficult to determine, but the vigilance of the rank and file seamen soon enough revealed the source of these rumors. Three thousand striking seamen, at a meeting at the Manhattan Lyceum, roared disapproval of the lies and rumors which had been circulated.

Prior to the calling of that meeting, in addition to the whispering campaign that the seamen were returning to their ships, an unrestrained attack upon the militant leaders of the strike was instituted. The newspapers in New York City and elsewhere generated a campaign against the influence of the Communist Party on the policy of the strike. The only prominent member of the Communist Party who served on the strike strategy committee was Al Lannon.

Agitation in advance of the meeting was directed towards an elimination of the influence of the Communists on the strike. The meeting not only rejected this campaign but proceeded to expose G. M. Skogman, a member of the strike strategy committee, as a stool pigeon and an agent of the shipowners.

A public trial was held at the meeting. Each member of the Strike Strategy Committee voluntarily placed himself as a target for any charges which the membership might wish to bring against him. One by one they stood trial and were re-elected unanimously. The entire committee, with the exception of Skogman, was re-elected and given a vote of confidence.

FINK BOOK FIGHT

Meanwhile the seamen had another fight on their hands—the fight against the fink book. During the latter part of January a mass delegation to Washington, representative of all of the ports, was organized. Some Congressmen protested the union-smashing provisions of the continuous discharge book and the continued granting of subsidies to shipowners.

On a cold and rainy night on February 11, 1938, around eleven o'clock, after a mass meeting at Stuyvesant High School, in New York City, striking seamen started their march on Washington. They were joined by delegations of rank and file seamen from Philadelphia and Baltimore. Boston sent a delegation. Senator Royal S. Copeland, author of the statute, and Secretary Roper, who inspired it, were both visited by the delegations. All that

Secretary Roper was able to say was "No one is forced to take the discharge book." Actually, the seamen could not sail without carrying one of these fink books.

The realization on the part of the seamen that their entire salvation lay in the ultimate repeal of this act, was a turning point in the Atlantic and Gulf strike. Perhaps the most dramatic expression of the unity of the merchant seamen was the heroic midnight march of the Baltimore brigade led by Patrick Whalen through rain and slush from that city all the way to the capitol, on foot.

On the morning of the arrival of the delegation in Washington, the writer was with a committee that visited in the office of Edward McGrady, the Assistant Secretary of Labor. That government official had received word of the arrival of the New York delegation and the march of the hungry, emaciated, embittered seamen from the port of Baltimore. He appealed to the committee in his office, asking that it stop the march on Washington because, as he stated, "Things are not done that way in Washington; you cannot move congressmen by mass marches and delegations. Stop it if you can. This demonstration cannot do the seamen any good!"

SPIRIT OF THE WORKERS

Well, the march was not stopped. The delegation arrived. Ultimately the law was repealed and the dog collar which was riveted around the neck of the American merchant seamen was removed by the indignation of an aroused group of workers. Yes, the East Coast and Gulf seamen returned to their ships without having won all of the demands and conditions for which they struggled. But out of that struggle came the conditions which are now being enjoyed by all of the merchant seamen. That struggle was carried on by workers who feared neither starvation nor sleet and storm along a waterfront in the dead of a winter's night. Seamen stood their watches on the picket line with the same determination that a seaman stands his watch in the stormiest weather at sea. Little did the returning strikers know that in less than five years they were to build a strong, powerful union that is an influence not only in the industry but in the nation at large.

But——and this too we must not forget——what is enjoyed today can be lost unless we remember the price that was paid for the conditions that are now enjoyed.

On May 1, in the spirit of our forefathers of 1776, all seamen on the Atlantic and Gulf coasts determined to burn their fink books, and as ships' crews tossed their fink books overboard, it became apparent that the dog collars could not continue around the necks of the seamen for long.

With promises of an amendment to the Fink Book law and the NLRB investigation, the strikers agreed to terminate the strike——except on intercoastal vessels, where it was to continue until a West Coast settlement was reached. (See Appendix.)

Chapter Eighteen

RADIO OPERATORS

The stirrings of organization among radio operators became manifest in the depths of the depression during the Hoover administration.

From the very first day that radio operators were placed upon merchant vessels, and up to 1931, the two watch system was maintained. Although on passenger vessels continuous radio service was maintained, only two operators were required. On passenger ships wages ranged from $50 to $100 a month for chief operators and from $40 to $80 per month for assistant radio operators. On freight vessels wages were even lower. These conditions stirred organization among maritime radio operators.

In March, 1931, there appeared the publication "*C.Q.*" This magazine was published by Mervin Rathborne, a West Coast unemployed radio operator. It was described as being published "of, by and for the commercial radio operators."

Simultaneously on the East Coast James J. Delaney founded the American Radio Association. The West Coast association, founded by Rathborne, was known as the Commercial Radiomen's Protective Association. In April 1932, ARA and CRPA were amalgamated. The new name of ARTA (American Radio Telegraphers

Association) was assumed and the total membership consisted of approximately 500 radio operators.

The nature of a radio man's work and the background of the persons then engaged in the craft led to the conception of their organization as a social club rather than a forthright labor organization. Although in the years since 1932 they have always been found in the front ranks of the struggles of militant workers, during the first few years of their life their activities could be characterized as defensive tactics.

FIRST STRIKE ACTION

In September, 1933, radio operators, for the first time, took strike action against the American Merchant Line, a subsidiary of the International Mercantile Marine, America's largest operator of merchant vessels. So little experience did the handful of radio operators have that in soliciting assistance from the officials of the then thriving Marine Workers Industrial Union, they asked such simple questions as "How do we walk on a picket line?"

It was a simple matter for the American Merchant Line to recruit scabs to sail the ships on time. The challenge taken up by these radio operators, as a result of their first experience, became an inspiration to other maritime workers.

Throughout the long, cold winter of 1933-34, ARTA members maintained picket lines before the piers and business offices of the American Merchant Line. Picketing in sub-zero weather, frequently without coats, arrests and continuous intimidation by the police soon enough convinced the radio operators that only through the establishment of a strong progressive and militant trade union could they improve their conditions and obtain wages commensurate with the skill required of them to be able to perform their tasks on board a vessel.

In September, 1934, the first national convention of the union was held. The discussion at this convention and the actions taken changed the whole philosophy of radio operators. It made clear to them that a united front of all marine workers was indispensable for success.

On November 10, 1933, Hoyt Haddock, the first president of ARTA, joined the Marine Workers Industrial Union representatives in appearances before the National Industrial Recovery Administration that was then holding hearings for the establishment of a code of fair practices and competition for the shipping industry.

Although during the maritime strike of 1934 ARTA did not have a sufficient number of members on the Pacific Coast to be able to give effective support or even officially to engage in the strike, the individual members of ARTA walked off their ships in sympathy with the strikers and gave all possible assistance to the striking crews.

The Maritime Federation of the Pacific Coast held its first convention at Seattle, Washington, in April, 1935. For the first time licensed officers, seamen, longshoremen, and radio operators were united in one organization. In the organization of the Maritime Federation of the Pacific, the officials of ARTA took an active part.

In September, 1935, the first general strike of radio operators took place on the Atlantic Coast. This strike was called after a referendum vote had been taken among the men who would be affected by it, and was supported by an overwhelming majority. The demands during this strike were:

1. Recognition of the union
2. Shipping through ARTA offices
3. Eight-hour working day
4. Wage increases

On the day that this strike was called, ARTA signed an agreement with the Radiomarine Corporation of America, which provided that the Radio Service Company would "nominate ARTA members for any job which became vacant on the 1100 ships which were under contract to carry RMCA radio equipment."

By the time the spring strike of 1936 was called, radio operators had already become veterans of the picket line and although quite close to topside, the radio operators appeared to have a greater kinship for the unlicensed personnel.

The main theme of the employers' publicity campaign during the 1936 strike was that the maritime unions were "reds" and that their leaders were "Communists" and "foreign agitators."

When the crew of the SS California, upon its discharge in New York on March 18, 1936, was greeted with scare headlines describing them as mutineers, the radio operators had already learned not to take too seriously such employer attacks.

The seamen who struck on the East Coast in the spring of 1936 were joined by many members of ARTA. Even though, as a result of their participation in this strike, many radio operators were left on the beach, locked out and blacklisted by the shipowners, they were not deterred from even more active militant participation in the fall and winter strike of 1936-37. They joined the unlicensed seamen in the spring of 1937 to wipe from the statute books the Copeland Fink Book law, which had been passed the previous year.

When the 1936-37 strike was over on the East Coast, between 350 and 400 ARTA members' jobs had been filled by scabs, and many of the ARTA strikers who had been on the picket lines for more than three months found themselves without jobs. But this discrimination was short-lived. The unlicensed seamen who, in May, 1937, organized the National Maritime Union on the East Coast did not forget the loyalty and selflessness of the radio operators during the cold winter days of 1936-37.

When, in April 1937, the radio operators kept the International Mercantile Marine liners *President Roosevelt* and *California* tied up in New York, and left the *SS City of Newport News* strikebound in Baltimore, the unlicensed seamen supported their strike action. As a result ARTA won from the IMM a closed shop agreement which provided the highest wages for radio operators ever secured by any union. It was thus that the radio operators acquired a fine understanding of the importance of unity with the unlicensed seamen.

The agreement between ARTA and IMM required the discharge of the scabs and the reinstatement to their jobs of the ARTA members. The success of the IMM radio operators was followed by strikes and job action which ARTA and the NMU conducted jointly during the spring of 1937. At that time, both the NMU and ARTA joined the CIO.

THIRD NATIONAL CONVENTION

The third national convention of ARTA took place in New York City in August, 1937. At this convention the total membership of ARTA was reported as being more than 4,000. Its members were organized in 41 locals, with the maritime local being one of the largest. It was at this convention that the name of the union was changed from American Radio Telegraphers Association to that of the American Communications Association, and thereafter the radio operators became known as the Marine Division of the ACA.

With the outbreak of war in 1939 and up to its termination in the spring of 1945, the heroism of radio operators was a source of inspiration to all men sailing merchant vessels.

Thereafter, in the summer of 1946, and again in 1947, whenever unlicensed seamen began to move to enforce their demands for the improvement of wages and working conditions, they knew they could always depend upon the militant support of radio operators. Every step taken to unify maritime workers found radio operators zealously supporting such action.

Chapter Nineteen

THE NMU IS BORN

After the strike, the members of the Sailors and Stewards Union decided to take steps to remove their reactionary officials and to put control of their union in the hands of the rank and file. A coastwise conference was called by the rank and file of both unions at which Joseph Curran, Frederick Myers and Charles DeGras for the sailors, and Ferdinand C. Smith, Gettlyn Lyons, and Frank Jones for the stewards, were elected as trustees for the Eastern and Gulf Sailors Association and the Marine Cooks and Stewards Union of the Atlantic and Gulf, respectively.

They were given the responsibility of carrying on negotiations with the International A. F. of L. Executive Board to bring about democratic elections of union officials.

In addition to this, the conference made the following proposals, in order to consolidate the gains resulting from the strike:

1. That the rank and file aboard the ships be built up and hold meetings on board the ships as often as possible.
2. That the position of the rank and file be explained to all seamen who had been confused by the disloyal elements put on board ships by the shipowners.

3. That they refuse to pay dues to the old line officials if they come aboard the ship and that no recognition be given to them.

4. That when in port, all union meetings be attended, and that all questions that arise on board ships be presented for the consideration of the membership at meetings.

5. That each pledge himself to force shipping through the union hall, and that the crews make it impossible for the shipowners to continue to employ through crimps.

6. That all minutes of meetings on board ships be forwarded to the rank and file trustees and officials and that all support be given to the *Pilot*.

During the latter part of April, 1937, the crew of the *SS President Roosevelt* struck in New York in support of two radio operators whose union rights the officials of the IMM had violated. The NLRB Regional Director, Mrs. Elinore M. Herrick, called a meeting at her office in an attempt to settle the strike without success. The meeting then adjourned to the home of John M. Franklin, President of the IMM. The rank and file officials of the MFOW and the trustees of the Eastern and Gulf Sailors Union represented the striking crews of all of the IMM ships.

RANK AND FILE RECOGNIZED

Before the meeting was adjourned the IMM agreed to recognize the rank and file representatives of their crews. The text of the agreement executed in the presence of the Regional Director before the crews sailed the ships was as follows:

1. Passes to board all IMM ships to be issued immediately to Rank and File delegates of the Sailors', Firemen's and Stewards' Unions.

2. Question of an election to determine proper bargaining agencies to be subject to joint conferences between representatives of the owners, representatives of the unions, and the National Labor Board. Such conferences to start immediately and every reasonable effort to be made to conclude them within ten days.

It is further understood between all parties that any election to designate any collective bargaining agency shall be conducted through the facilities of the National Labor Relations Board.

3. All IMM ships now tied up shall be sailed at once.

4. This agreement was entered between the American Radio Telegraphists Association, the MFOW, and the IMM, and the terms of the agreement agreed upon by all parties.

The crews on IMM ships were determined to protect their interests and a large number of sit-down strikes took place. All of these acts looked towards the recognition by the shipowners of the rank and file officials in place of the old line officials.

By May 4, the IMM had agreed to hire men from the new central headquarters established by the rank and file seamen at 126 Eleventh Avenue, New York City. The Munson Line followed suit and all crews were advised to insist on being hired only through the union hall.

NMU ORGANIZED

It was becoming obvious that even though the overwhelming majority of the East Coast seamen supported the rank and file officials, the ISU officialdom did not relinquish their control of the union, and, therefore, in order to protect themselves, the seamen would have to organize their own union outside the ISU.

Following the strike, the National Labor Relations

Board agreed to hold an election within the union. The Firemen's Union was not to be included because their election had been sustained in the highest court. However, the old line officials challenged the Board's jurisdiction on the ground that the Wagner Act authorized the Board to hold an election to determine the collective bargaining representatives only in instances where a labor dispute existed.

To hurdle this opposition, a delegation of rank and file seamen's representatives appeared before a full AFL Executive Council meeting to petition it to conduct an election within the ISU under the supervision of a member of the Executive Council.

At the end of the meeting a committee of three council members, headed by Matthew Woll, was designated to supervise and conduct such an election. The ISU officials, who saw themselves about to be deprived of their lifelong jobs, sabotaged even this proposal. Finally, however, the rank and file recognized that only through continued united action could they achieve ultimate emancipation—and on May 5, 1937, they organized their own union, the National Maritime Union.

NEW TRUSTEES

The trustees in behalf of both the Maritime Cooks and Stewards Union of the Atlantic and Gulf and the Eastern and Gulf Sailors' Association submitted a joint report on their efforts to obtain recognition of the democratic rights of representative membership and to secure elections to determine the collective bargaining agents of the seamen. It was pointed out that the steamship companies were then already recognizing the emergency officials which the rank and file had elected. Furthermore, the payment of dues also left no room for doubt that the majority of the membership of the unions considered the trustees and other emergency officials as their duly elected representatives.

The steamship companies expressed their willingness to recognize representatives elected by the seamen through an election held under the auspices of the NLRB. The AFL Executive Council had done everything in its power to frustrate the holding of an NLRB election, and since the old line officials had obtained a court order preventing the rank and file seamen from using the name Marine Cooks and Stewards' Union, it became necessary for the rank and file seamen of the ISU to authorize their elected officials to adopt a name other than that of the ISU.

It was therefore proposed that the trustees of the sailors and cooks unions become the provisional officers of NMU until new elections could be held and that these provisional officers of the NMU be instructed to propose to all seafaring unions on the East, West and Gulf coasts to convene a National Unity Convention of the maritime workers.

CIO BECKONS

Within a week after this resolution was adopted the duly elected officials of the MFOW joined the Sailors' and Cooks' unions in the organization of a national union. John Brophy, director of the CIO, then conferred with representatives of the National Maritime Union and advised them that the doors of the CIO were open to them. By May 21 the Standard Oil Company of New Jersey had agreed to issue passes to delegates. The Company also recognized the Engine Division, formerly the

MFOW. In the meantime in every port along the Atlantic and Gulf coasts, similar action was taken.

The wonder of all wonders now occurred! With all of the East Coast and Gulf seamen unanimously behind the rank and file seamen, the ISU through their old line officials filed a petition with the NLRB alleging that a question had arisen concerning the representation of the unlicensed personnel employed by more than fifty steamship companies. The provisional officers of the NMU heartily welcomed this petition by the ISU and within less than a week's time consented to an election.

To create unity between the various crafts, in June 1937 the New York Maritime Council was organized. The following organizations composed the council: National Maritime Union; Mates and Pilots; Marine Engineers' Beneficial Association; American Radio Telegraphists' Association; Industrial Union of Marine and Shipbuilding Workers; Apprentice Engineers' Association; Scandinavian Seamen's Club; and Lumber Workers Union.

It was the intention of the labor unions who organized this council to sponsor similar councils in other cities along the Atlantic and Gulf, which organizations ultimately would organize a Maritime Federation of the Atlantic and Gulf.

LAKES DRIVE PLAN

At the same time that the New York Council was organized, officials of the NMU met in Washington with officials of the Committee for Industrial Organization on the question of an organizational drive among the Lakes seamen. While these campaigns to organize the unorganized and create unity among the maritime unions were going on, the provisional officers of the unions called a constitutional convention of the National Maritime Union.

This convention met July 12. Prior to the meeting, a great deal of serious consideration was given to the character of the organization. All were agreed that an industrial union in which all three crafts were united without regard to craft division would be most desirable. As far back as 1922 such a proposal had been introduced at an ISU convention. Obviously, the delegate to the ISU convention, each of whom was an official of a district union, would not accede to a merger of all three divisions. The delegates at the 1922 convention were not rank and filers.

On the other hand, the craft division had been in effect on board ships for so long a time that it was doubtful whether it was possible to eradicate the craft division with a stroke of the pen or even a unanimous vote of all delegates in support.

During the heat of the strike, a movement was set afoot to have the stewards meet separately during the strike. One of the leaders of the movement was Joseph Murphy, later expelled from the union for shipowners' connections. A proposal to act as a craft unit actually was considered by the striking stewards at a meeting held in New York, but its splitting character was exposed by Ferdinand C. Smith, a former chief steward.

DEMOCRATIC CONSTITUTION

Almost one hundred constitutions were examined before the skeleton of the new constitution was even reduced to paper. Constitutions of marine firemen dating back to 1902 were examined, as was the constitution of the National Sailors' and Firemen's Union of Great Britain and Ireland. *One principle that was foremost in the minds of the drafters of the constitution was the need for an instrument which would protect the rank and file against the possible encroachment by their own elected officials upon their democratic rights, and the need for simple machinery to remove an officer if, in the opinion of the rank and file, he failed properly to perform his duties.*

The democratic character of the convention was shown by a report of the Credentials Committee: 118 ships were represented by 136 delegates; 14 ports were represented by 68 delegates. And in addition, there were 14 alternate port delegates and two alternate ship delegates.

A number of fraternal delegates attended from various organizations to observe the forming of this great union. Among these were representatives from the West Coast MFOW, the ILD, the American Radio Telegraphers Association, the Sailors Union of the Pacific, and the Canadian Seamen's Union.

Only a convention whose delegates represented so completely the working membership on board the ships would have evolved the instrument which it did. The drafts of the constitution were submitted to the membership for ratification, and thereafter elections were ordered for the first officers to serve the membership under the newly adopted constitution.

Chapter Twenty

ATTACK FROM WITHIN

With the first constitutional convention completing its business at the end of July, 1937, a whirlwind campaign was instituted really to organize the unorganized. The provisional officers of the union toured the Gulf area, the Great Lakes, and the Atlantic coast. Others toured the rivers.

The New York Maritime Council at the same time carried on a campaign to organize harbor workers. The *Pilot* inaugurated a campaign to expose the ILA as the corrupt counterpart of the ISU. The vile corruption within that organization, even to this day, has not been fully exposed. In the Gulf area the rank and file representatives carried on a day-to-day campaign to organize the inland workers. In this campaign the national organization of the CIO co-operated.

In the Great Lakes, three companies recognized the NMU as the collective bargaining representatives—Great Lakes Transit Corporation, Interstate Steamship Company (Jones and Laughlin fleet), and Midland Steel fleet. These companies were members of the notorious anti-labor Lake Carriers Association, and the NMU felt that it had indeed scored a definite victory in getting this preliminary recognition from the companies. The first meeting with the Transit Corporation officials took place during the last week of September. More than ample evidence was offered that the NMU had organized the crews of the vessels owned by these companies. The agreement which was presented to these three companies was based on the agreement which had already been signed with the Minnesota-Atlantic Transport Co., known as the "Poker Fleet" because its ships were named Ace, King, Queen, Jack, etc.

OTHER COMPANIES SIGN

In the meantime, on the East Coast, Joseph Curran, Ferdinand C. Smith, and Moe Byne of the district committee brought nine East Coast Collier Companies in line. An agreement was signed covering the unlicensed 2,240 men employed on 56 vessels which were operated by the following companies: Mystic Steamship Co., M. & J. Tracy, Inc., Coastwise Transportation Co., New England and Southern Steamship Co., Diamond Transportation Co., Staples Coal Co., Pocahontas Steamship Co., Hartwelson Steamship Co. and the Wellhart Steamship Co.

On January 14, 1938, the Tanker Negotiating Committee and the members of the District Committee reported that the Standard Oil Company of New Jersey had signed the tanker agreement at its offices. This agreement covered 17,000 merchant seamen employed on approximately 300 vessels. It was designed to cover the whole industry operating tankers on the Atlantic and Gulf coasts, and made positive improvements of the conditions of the seamen.

The salient points of this agreement were:

1. Three weeks annual vacation with full pay for the un-

licensed personnel, with the option of ten days every six months.

2. Five-dollar increase in monthly wages, representing a total increase for the industry of nearly $1,000,000 in cash in the pockets of the seamen.

3. Improved living conditions and vastly improved working conditions on all the companies signatory to the agreement.

4. Preferential employment for members of the National Maritime Union at all times.

5. Seventy-five cents per hour for overtime.

6. An arbitration provision which provides for the peaceful, just, and speedy settlement of all disputes that may arise in connection with the agreement.

7. Agreement goes into effect April 1, 1938, and expires April 1, 1939, thus bringing a large section of our agreements up close to the summer months.

Members of the committee were frank enough to point out some of the weaknesses of the agreement. They recognized that they had not procured the 100 per cent closed shop and possibly had not obtained as great a monthly increase in pay as they had hoped. But these shortcomings, it was felt, could easily be overcome at the end of the year when the agreement came up for renewal—after the membership had had an opportunity to consolidate their strength. This agreement was signed, in addition to the Standard Oil Company of New Jersey, by the following: Socony-Vacuum Oil Co., Gulf Oil Corp., the Texas Company, Sinclair Refining Co., Pennsylvania Oil Co., C. D. Mallory & Co., Pure Oil Co., Richfield Oil Co., Continental Oil Co., and others.

WINNING NLRB ELECTIONS

In the meantime, the results of the NLRB elections, which had been begun during the previous year, revealed that the seamen voluntarily supported the NMU as the choice between this newly organized union and the International Seamen's Union of America.

The following is only a partial list indicating the character of this choice:

	NMU	ISU
Standard Oil Co. of New Jersey	1703	46
New York & Cuba Mail	572	20
Cities Service Oil Co.	234	78
Grace Lines	765	14
Munson Steamship Co.	774	42
The Export Steamship Corp.	656	16
American West African Lines	183	3
Lykes Bros. Steamship Co.	1049	10
The Texas Company	431	54

In several instances the NMU was the unanimous choice of the crews. Crews of the American Foreign Steamship Company, the Kellogg Steamship Corporation, the Standard Fruit and Steamship Company, and the American Sugar Transit Corporation did not cast a single vote in favor of the ISU.

The shipowners, in the face of this unanimous choice, decided to resort to their old technique of destroying the union from within, sending their agents and stool pigeons right into the heart of the union and wherever possible securing for them official positions in the top ranks of the union leadership.

That the shipowners had used this technique before first became evident when Skogman was exposed in the midst of the strike. During the strike, a steward by the name of Joseph Murphy persuaded the stewards to hire a hall of their own. At this meeting, referred to in the preceding chapter, Murphy arose and complained of the "top-heavy" character of the strike strategy committee. He called for a single leader (a fuehrer), who alone would be responsible for the leadership of the strike. After the NMU was organized, Murphy was exposed as an agent of Joseph P. Ryan. The extent to which Murphy and Skogman had "hooked" a good many of the rank and file leaders we were to learn in the future.

At any rate, within less than a month after it was submitted the tanker agreement was signed. As soon as ratification had taken place, three delegates, Kenneth Warner from the Deck Division, Eddie Choquette from the Engine Division, and Octave Loones from the Stewards Division, sent in their resignations. They gave their reasons for resigning in almost identical language. They said that the agreement was unworthy.

RANK AND FILE PILOT APPEARS

But lo and behold on March 1, 1938, there appeared on the waterfront a four-page publication described as *The Rank and File NMU Pilot*. Octave Loones blossomed out as its editor and the entire issue was devoted to an attack upon the tanker agreement as a document enslaving the seamen. The sum and substance of their complaint was that the contract did not contain a closed-shop provision.

This *Pilot* came regularly every two weeks and, in spite of the protest that it was being solely supported by the contributions of rank and file seamen, became larger and was printed on costlier paper. Each succeeding issue engaged in minute attacks upon each individual official of the Union, except a few officials who within less than a year were to be exposed as shipowner agents.

During the month of March, ballots for election of officers went to all ports, and the *Rank and File Pilot* began its campaign against the leading officials of the union.

Balloting for officials took place during April and May. The shipowners were using every trick at their command to influence the vote of the membership. At both division and joint meetings, disruption regularly took place. Members appeared on the waterfront wearing white buttons with seagulls on them. The wearers of these buttons openly admitted that they were members of what is known as the Mariners Club, and a great many of these Mariners Club members were distributing what came to be known as the "Red, White, and Blue" ballots. This was a facsimile of the official ballot printed in blue ink on white paper with tiny red "hammer and sickle" insignias besides the names of candidates unacceptable to the shipowners.

After the voting, the *Rank and File Pilot* disappeared from the waterfront. Apparently the shipowners had intended to use it but for one purpose: to influence the vote of the membership. Octave Loones, for reasons to be explained later, ceased being the editor of the *Pilot* after the first three issues. He was succeeded by one William L. Holler.

Results of the counting were published in the official *Pilot* each week. The candidates in whom the shipowners were interested, it soon became clear, were the following: Jerome King, Frederick C. Phillips, Sherman Lemmon, Arthur Thomas, C. J. Applewhite, and George Hearn. Hearn was later absolved of any complicity in the activities of the Mariners Club or of the *Rank and File Pilot* crowd.

THE BASEBALL BAT RAIDS

In the *Pilot* of July 29 Moe Byne was leading George Hearn for the office of Atlantic District treasurer by a little more than 100 votes. It stood at 6,106 for Byne and 5,974 for Hearn. In the Gulf, the Mariners Club candidate, C. J. Applewhite, was also running behind Robert Meers for the office of Gulf District secretary-treasurer, 1,834 to 2,063.

The last port to be counted was Galveston, where more than 2,000 ballots had been cast. Obviously these ballots would determine the election for the two sharply contested offices.

Under the constitution there were nine judges of election whose duty it was to count the 20,000 or more ballots. Since there were 282 candidates, obviously it was almost impossible for all nine judges to count each ballot. The judges, therefore, divided the ballots among themselves to speed the count.

In the ballot room, votes that were being called out in favor of Byne were discovered being marked by some of the judges of election in the Hearn column. What took place in the ballot room that day was fully described by Howard McKenzie when he testified later at the trial of Jerome King:

I walked into the balloting room and stood by Germach and Blackwell [two of the judges]. Germach was calling out the votes and Blackwell was tallying them with a large black pencil. Naturally, as Germach picked up each ballot I would look and there was usually a cross marked for Byne—and anybody could see the port was going for Byne.

So Germach would call out "Byne" and Blackwell would mark a dash next to Hearn. I stood there and watched for about twenty minutes and I couldn't believe my eyes at first. It was simply too raw.

Suddenly, Bill Cunningham, Bob Maren, and somebody else came running in and told us to get the hell out. "Red" Hawks, now a patrolman in Boston, was also present. "Scotty" Edwards had already been dumped that morning for making objections about the ballots.

One of them said, "Close that door and give it to them." Blackwell jumped over the table and started working Byne over. Byne made no attempt to defend himself. He said later he didn't want to fight back and have the whole thing disrupted and some of the ballots destroyed.

Cunningham and somebody else went to work on "Red" Hawkes, beating him to the floor and kicking him under the table. [The presence of Cunningham and Maren in the ballot room was a violation of the constitution inasmuch as neither was a candidate.] Just prior to the raid, the elevator operator had slipped into the ballot room and put three small baseball bats in the corner.

No attempt was made to dump me at that time. Somebody opened the door and said: "Now all you bastards get out of here or we'll bring in the baseball bats next time." Byne and I went to the second floor. Byne's face was all marked up and several members asked him what had happened. I told them what I thought in strong language: that the shipowners were trying to take over the union and that there were people here who were paid by the operators and were nothing but cheap gangsters and were trying to take over the organization with baseball bats.

I came up to the fifth floor with a hundred men or so and was going to demand a recount of the Galveston ballots. As we came on to the fifth floor, Joe Curran stepped off the elevator and wanted to know what the commotion was about. Well, I was pretty hot. I didn't recall where King was at this particular time, but Curran walked into the ballot room and asked what the trouble was.

They told him that the judges of the election were being interfered with in their duty. He told them that if they would recount the first hundred ballots from Galveston it would probably stop the commotion. . . .

"Well, it's going to look mighty funny that you refused to recount such a small number of ballots," Curran said. "Something must be wrong. It's a damn sight better for the union that they be counted now and save the expense of a whole recount later on."

"Nothing doing," Ashton said again.

"You won't count them over?" Joe asked.

"No."

When I came out of the ballot room about five minutes later, King was in the outside office. I asked him then: "How can you, an official of the union, sit there and watch all this go on. Who is responsible for this?" King's reply was for me not to start anything I couldn't finish.

This brazen decision to disregard the solemn expression of membership through a secret ballot was soon discovered to be only the beginning of a long series of abuses. Shortly after this episode described by McKenzie, during a fire drill that was being conducted in the building, a group of men flourishing baseball bats began to bang on desks and walls, going through all the offices, forcing office workers and union officials to drop what they were doing. Only the presence of mind of some of the rank and file officials of the union stopped actual bloodshed at that time. It was not inconceivable that the baseball bat goons were sent by the enemies from without in the hope that blood would be shed. That, fortunately, did not occur.

CURRAN'S LETTER TO THE MEMBERSHIP

After this episode, Joseph Curran addressed the following letter to the membership:

Dear Brothers: In the past few weeks, many things have taken place of which the membership in the various ports and on board the ships are probably not aware.

The elections are drawing to a close and as a result of the close vote in some instances a group of twenty or thirty have set themselves up in a desperate attempt to destroy the union. The union headquarters was raided by this group, most of whom are members of the National Maritime Union: The bookkeepers and stenographers were driven from the headquarters last Thursday afternoon, and in some cases threatened with bodily harm. Certain officials in the union were also driven from the union offices.

This group took the position that they were going to drive all the Communists out of the union, in spite of the fact that the officials had been elected by the membership up and down the coast, and the constitution states that there shall be no discrimination for political belief; they still take the position that a local group has the right to dictate as to who are and who are not going to be the officials of this union.

Meetings have broken up in riots and have been disrupted completely by this group on the pretext of cleaning out the Communists. Many bona fide seamen have been attacked because they disagreed with this group or tried to take the floor. This presents a very serious problem to the union. It means that we, the membership, must decide definitely, once and for all—is the union to be run by the rank and file membership on a coastwise basis or is it to be dominated by a local group or clique in the port of New York?

The newspapers have been carrying stories of a split in the NMU, even going so far as to say that there is a "Right Wing" faction in the union, led by Jerome King, fighting against Curran who they claim is going down the line with the Communists, and using this as an excuse to continue their terror.

In my opinion the membership should take steps to see why this union reign of terror against the officials is being carried on. Because of this reign of terror we have not been able to do any of the work which we were elected to do, such as fighting the Maritime Commission fink halls; the training bills which are now becoming a fact; negotiations with the shipowners; and numerous other details, which it is our duty to handle.

It appears to me that the excuse that is being used by these people, that of ousting the Communists from the union, is only a smokescreen for their efforts to destroy the union because they cannot dominate it. Unless the membership takes a hand in this situation and decides as to how they want their union run, this group can be the means of destroying the union. That is the way the ISU was run and why it was destroyed.

We cannot, we must not tolerate any attempt on the part of any groups to destroy this union and to drive us back to the conditions we had to endure under the ISU. It is my opinion that this movement is being sponsored by someone behind the scenes of the AFL.

It has already been stated by this group that they are going to move in, in spite of the fact that the general election, in which thousands of members participated, may have designated some officials who did not please this group. They have threatened to drive such officials out of office or force them to resign.

Editorials are appearing in the newspapers pointing out that the union is breaking up and that these groups are fighting the Communists. They are fighting what they claim to be Communists, but at the same time, every progressive member who takes the floor and disagrees with their policy is subject to being beaten up and run off the waterfront. This publicity is obviously not intended to help the prestige of the union.

The shipowners do not want to negotiate agreements because they say there is a split in the union, although we know there isn't a split, but merely an attempt to control or destroy the union. This union will not be destroyed if the membership do not allow themselves to be misled by any group or clique that attempts to use them for their own ends.

I point these things out so that you may all have an idea of what is taking place on the waterfront. It is your job to see that your union is run in a clean democratic manner and that no groups or cliques are allowed to dominate it.

It is up to you as members of the union to decide whether or not you are going to allow baseball bats to run your union or whether it is going to be run democratically with the right of every member to his own beliefs, so long as they do not interfere with the policies of the union.

Don't be played for suckers. The officials will stand on their past record. If it can be shown that they sold you out, you have democratic constitutional ways and means to oust them and you don't have to resort to baseball bat disruption which is exactly what the AFL and the shipowners would like to see you do.

Chapter Twenty-one

SHIPOWNER SPIES EXPOSED

Early in September, 1938, after the election results were out, the writer received a call from Octave Loones asking for a conference. It was arranged and for several hours Loones narrated a weird story of corruption, larceny, and labor-spy activities. Had Senator LaFollette's investigation not already exposed labor-spy activities on the part of outstanding corporations, the Loones narrative could easily have been taken for that of an irrational person. In spite of the fact that he had resigned as a delegate of the MCS in 1936 and helped the rank and file in their action against Grange, the writer was unwilling to accept his story as worthy of belief. Later Loones, at the suggestion of the writer, prepared an affidavit which he submitted to the LaFollette Committee. This affidavit deserves being published in full:

November 7, 1938

Octave Loones, being duly sworn, deposes and says:

I served as an organizer for the National Maritime Union until February 4, 1938, at which time I resigned. On March 15, 1938, I was expelled from the National Maritime Union because of my activities with the publication of a weekly paper known as the *Rank and File Pilot*.

Rank and File Pilot was a weekly paper which was founded by myself and Jerry King, who was at that time secretary of the Seamen's Union in New York, which subsequently became the National Maritime Union.

Jerry King was also elected as secretary-treasurer of the National Maritime Union after it was formed. I published the *Rank and File Pilot* because I was dissatisfied with the leadership of the National Maritime Union.

I was principally dissatisfied with the contract which had been signed in February, 1938, covering the seamen in the tanker division.

The first issue of the *Rank and File Pilot* appeared on March 1, 1938, and was prepared by myself and Jerry King. Jerry King turned over to me about $186 for the purpose of defraying the cost of the publication.

After preparing the first edition of the *Rank and File Pilot*, Jerry King and I took into our group Sherman Lemmon, who is now serving with the United States Maritime Commission as a personnel representative. We also took in Walter Carney, who was secretary of the deck division of the National Maritime Union.

In the middle of March, I was living in an apartment on the third floor of a house located on 87th Street in Brooklyn, above a saloon. Someone in the saloon brought me a message to call Mr. Stanley at AShland 4-1390.

I went to the public telephone in the saloon and called the number. A voice at the other end asked me to identify myself and to give the number of the phone from which I was calling. I was then told to hang up. Immediately, I received a call back to my telephone and a voice at the other end of the wire stated that he was Mr. Stanley.

He said that he was a Reserve Officer of the United States Naval Intelligence. Mr. Stanley stated that he was opposed to communistic influences among the seamen and that he was in favor of the work that I was doing through the *Rank and File Pilot*. Mr. Stanley said that he had documents which he would be glad to make available to me.

He then discussed the work and showed complete famili-

arity with the activities of myself, King, Carney, and Lemmon. Mr. Stanley said that it would not be convenient for
me to come to his home or office, but he was willing to come
to my house that evening and I therefore asked him to do so.

He arrived later that evening with a man named Ray
Carlucci, a man with dark brown hair, who at one time lived
in Montclair, New Jersey, but who, it later developed, was
living with Mr. Stanley at the Commodore Hotel.

I had previously met Carlucci sometime in February at
the house of a friend of mine named Bernard Weston, who
at the time was working on the SS *Eagle,* operated by the
Esso Vacuum Company.

Mr. Stanley brought with him documents which he offered
to make available to us. One of these documents, which is
attached hereto as Exhibit A*, is a photostat of the minutes
of the Great Lakes Conference of February 3, 1938. A second
document, which is attached hereto as Exhibit B*, was a two-
page typewritten report on the finances of the National Maritime Union.

That evening I discussed with Mr. Stanley the principles
and purposes of our organization and he stated that he
desired to co-operate with us fully and suggested that I call
him daily at his number for the purpose of receiving information or suggestions.

I called up Mr. Stanley every day at around two o'clock
and exchanged information with him. I also saw him frequently. As part of the campaign against the leadership of
the union, we organized the Mariners' Club, which formed
the center of our activities.

Sherman Lemmon originally took charge of organizing
these clubs. Charges were circulated, however, that he was
dictatorial. I understand that these charges originated from
Ray Carlucci. At any rate, Lemmon retired from active
work in connection with the Mariners' Club and Carlucci
took over control of the club.

* Exhibits referred to above are not available to the writer.

On May 27, 1938, a crisis developed in our organization because of a conflict between the National Maritime Union and the Sailors' Union of the Pacific over representation on the lines of the Shepard Steamship Company.

As a result of this conflict, the sentiment among the seamen in the National Maritime Union was to support the regular officers, and this was losing the insurgent group led by the *Rank and File Pilot* a large number of the followers.

Carlucci called for myself and King at the printing shop and drove us to the Commodore Hotel at 3:30 in the afternoon to discuss the matter with Mr. Stanley. We went to room 1934, and found Mr. Stanley there accompanied by a man whom I recognized as Mr. J. A. Jump. Later in the day Walter Carney joined us in the room.

King left in the afternoon to attend a meeting of the executive board of the union downtown and he returned later at about 7:30 P.M. to continue the discussion. We had liquor and meals served in the room and spent the entire evening discussing the matter.

Mr. J. A. Jump, I recognized as a company official holding some position with the Isthmian Line, which is a subsidiary of the United States Steel Corporation.

As a result of discussing the situation, we agreed that it would be advantageous to our group to have the dispute between the NMU and the Sailors' Union of the Pacific settled as speedily as possible so that we could continue our attack on the leaders of the union without appearing to be disloyal to the organization.

Mr. Jump, therefore, made a long distance call to Pittsburgh and spoke to somebody named "Mac" and said to him, "Get your men busy in 'Frisco to put the screws on Lundberg to call off the fight."

During the discussion in the room, Jump called Stanley "Jim." Jump also whispered to Stanley with reference to paying for a long distance call to Pittsburgh and Stanley replied, "That's all right, I'll put in on my expense account."

These remarks as well as the presence of Jump aroused my suspicions about Mr. Stanley.

The following day I called up Stanley at the Commodore and asked for room 1934 and was told that "Mr. Walsh did not answer." I later called the regular number at ASland 4-1390 and asked for "Jim."

I was told to call WHitehall 4-2180 and ask for extension No. 51. When I called WHitehall 4-2180, the switchboard operator replied, "Isthmian Steamship Line" and upon asking for extension No. 51, I was connected with Mr. Stanley.

My suspicions were thoroughly aroused at this point and having heard gossip about detective agencies operating among seamen, I secured a Red Book and looked through the list of detective agencies.

My eye was struck by a large advertisement of the Harry J. O'Connor Detective Agency located at some address on 110th Street with the telephone number AShland 4-1390. I then went and found Jerry King and told him that Mr. Stanley was, in fact, a detective named Jim Walsh, and that he was apparently connected with the United States Steel Company's Steamship Line.

I also pointed out that Ray Carlucci appeared to be his employee, because Stanley had frequently stated that he and Carlucci had worked together for about ten years, and Carlucci was playing an important part in controlling our organization.

I, therefore, suggested that I should meet with him and King and Lemmon and that the four of us should take some steps to shake ourselves loose of the detectives that had taken up with us.

King answered frankly that he knew Carlucci and Walsh were detectives but that if we exposed them it would discredit our organization. He further advised me to take no action and said that "you are too far in it now to squawk."

In the meantime, the National Maritime Union had called a port holiday to take effect on June 2, as a means of retaliating against the Sailors' Union of the Pacific.

Without consulting me, Walsh, King, Carlucci, Hennessey, Innes, and the others had put out fifteen thousand multigraphed leaflets advising the men not to participate in the strike.

I had loaned some money to Walsh or Stanley which I wished to get back. As an excuse for not paying me the money, Walsh said that he had paid for the fifteen thousand leaflets which had been distributed. He showed me the receipt for the work. I was accompanied by two men named Galagher and Stighlitz, who also saw the receipt.

After I had spoken to Jerry King and he had refused to take any action with reference to Stanley and Carlucci, I wrote a letter to the printer and informed him that I would no longer be responsible for any obligations incurred in connection with the publication of the *Rank and File Pilot*.

ACTIVITIES OF CARLUCCI AND KING

The *Rank and File Pilot* spoke openly of the activities of an official of the Isthmian Steamship Company and of a detective by the name of James A. Walsh who operated an "industrial service." Carlucci and King's activities were referred to as follows:

The mystery surrounding Carlucci and Stanley, who meanwhile had changed his name to Duffy, had been getting under my skin and made me quite uncomfortable, consequently when Jerry King brought Carlucci within our group I asked what his business was or what part he was playing in this picture.

King's answer to this was that he was a rank and filer and belonged to the engine division of the NMU and was OK, merely a good fellow out of a job, owning a car, and who played chauffeur to King whenever he had to go somewhere in a hurry, and in this fashion could cultivate King's confidence and learn what transpired in the district committee.

Chapter Twenty-two

"PAY-OFF" MEN

After Loones' exposure, King, Carlucci, Hennessey, Walter Carney and other officials who were close to this group, as well as the unofficial cabinet working under them, became more and more brazen. Young Peter J. Innes, Jr., who had been designated by King as a purchasing agent, was discovered paying much more for certain printing bills than appeared justifiable. Walter Carney, in turn, became so bold that he issued union books illegally to seamen who undoubtedly were to carry out their program on board ships, and moneys received for such books were not turned in by him to the union treasury.

Finally, he was arrested, and immediately he wrote a series of threatening letters to John L. Lewis, Lee Pressman, and the writer, all of which correspondence, of course, was forwarded to the union's president. Carney, apparently, had hoped that by making threats of exposure he would obtain from the shipowners that financial and moral support which he needed so badly to obtain his release from prison.

CARNEY TALKS

Finally, recognizing that his threats were getting him nowhere, Carney agreed to talk. And talk he did! A series of letters were written by him and mailed from the Tombs Prison to the writer which, too, deserve being published in full:

The union officials and steamship officials who are involved to sabotage the union and break the agreement and swing the NMU into the AFL:

Taylor of Institute (formerly ASOA).

NAMES OF PAY-OFF MEN FOR SHIPOWNERS

Companies	SS Official	NMU Official
Standard Oil	R. Hague Taylor, P.O.M.*	J. King F. Phillips
Luckenbach SS Co	Singleton Comeford, P.O.M.*	J. King F. Phillips S. Lemmon
Grace Line	Tom Mann, P.O.M.*	J. King S. Lemmon
Isthmian SS Co	Capt. Jump Ray Carlucci, P.O.M.*	J. King S. Lemmon Hennessey Loones F. Steglich
Railroad Audit Co		F. Steglich Hennessey J. King Loones

*Pay-off men.

These contacts were made before the Standard Oil agreement and a thousand dollars were passed to J. King and S. Lemmon in the Standard Oil office on the 22nd floor of Radio City, on their promise to sabotage the oil agreement and change the leadership as they wanted Jack Lawrenson out of the way.

Frederick Phillips came into the picture through the American Legion and met Hague and Co. and sat in on the conferences in the George Washington Hotel where the red and black ballot was born and fifteen hundred dollars were passed to concentrate on the elections. At the next meeting at the George Washington Hotel on the 23rd the *Rank and File Pilot* was born and also the Mariners' Club. At that meeting was R. Hague, Taylor of the Institute, Capt. Jump, Singleton and Tom Mann. The NMU was represented by S. Lemmon, J. King, F. Phillips and myself and a financial arrangement amongst the groups was provided to handle the funds, Taylor for the SS owner group, Lemmon and King for the NMU.

The start of the *Rank and File Pilot* was provided material through the Railroad Audit Co. and Ray Carlucci working for Big Steel and the Isthmian Line.

Capt. Jump and members of the Railroad Audit Co. met Loones and Hennessey, and naturally every time we met the food and liquor flowed.

The contents of the *Rank and File Pilot* are mostly accurate in names, places, date. [This is the issue containing Loones' statement.]

Joe Ryan was dickering with J. King for William Green, AFL, and Harry Lundeberg to swing the NMU to the AFL. That was after J. King promised to Harry Lundeberg at the Cornish Arms Hotel to swing the NMU to H. Lundeberg if he would produce the money and gorillas to swing it; that was in the summer of 1937.

At the meeting of the inner circle of Mariners' Club after the Loones exposures at Gallagher's house, J. King decided to let the Mariners' Club die a natural death. The cash was stopped, and it died itself as nobody was paid and had to be disbanded.

The Mariners' Club was supported and formed at that

meeting in the George Washington Hotel and the *Rank and File Pilot* idea was born.

The money actually stopped when Ray Carlucci was put on trial and found guilty and when nobody was producing for Standard Oil and companies.

Carlucci was working for big steel and the Railroad Audit Co., with headquarters in the Commodore Hotel at that time.

The George Washington Hotel was the meeting place for the shipowners.

Hennessey was naturally working with King, Carlucci, and the Signal Printing Co., of whom he received a four per cent rake-off on all printing. With Loones, Hennessey was editor of the *Rank and File Pilot*. He met Capt. Jump a few times in hotel and received material and information from Railroad Audit Co.

Frederick Phillips is contact for the American Legion on un-American ideas and came into contact with Standard Oil the same time as we did but through the American Legion and Railroad Audit Co.

(signed) Walter Carney.

Here is Carney's *second* letter:

There were four meetings held with the Steamship Owners, one meeting with R. Hague in Radio City and the other three with SS owners in the George Washington Hotel.

The meeting was switched from Radio City to the George Washington Hotel because naturally nobody wanted to be recognized in the Standard Oil Office.

As you go into the George Washington Hotel, Lexington Avenue entrance into the lobby, turn left to staircase and up to first floor, turn right and the first door on the left private banquet room with bar is caucus room.

After formalities were over and the Scotch and grub started to flow, J. King—S. Lemmon—F. Phillips were asked what they could offer.

Their offer in return for financial help was to get rid of
the un-American element during elections and sabotage oil
contract and also to get rid of Jack Lawrenson at any cost.

They were asked by what method, and the Red & Black
ballot was born. It was tentatively agreed at that time to use
strong arm methods with outsiders coming in with NMU
books.

At later meeting the idea of outside help and strong arm
influence was vetoed and the method of recruiting for the
Mariners' Club was set up and a method devised to get a
newspaper out on the style of the *Pilot* to be known as the
Rank and File Pilot.

Carl Lynch, editor of the ISU seamen journal, was contacted and then Jump came into the picture with a caucus
at the Commodore Hotel, J. King, Lemmon, Phillips, also
Phillips' friend from the American Legion, who turned out
to belong to the Railroad Audit Co. Agency.

After talking with Carl Lynch & Co. the idea of being
editor was vetoed; and Loones or Hennessey were to be
asked to be editor. The editor is *Rank and File Pilot* history;
he helped in its formation and setup but Carl Lynch had to
drop out of the picture when the regular *Pilot* showed the
setup of both papers being printed in the same shop as the
Seamen Journal AFL-ISU.

The last meeting in the George Washington Hotel, Mr. R.
Hague & Co. had pooled their money with R. Hague as pay
off man for the steamship owners and J. King as collector
for our group. It was thought best after arrangements had
all been made to discontinue the meetings at the hotel and
to produce as per agreement and arrangements as detection
was possible and were a-scared of being seen together.

Naturally, plans were made to gather material, set up the
club, and start the ballot and newspaper *Rank and File Pilot*,
and set the campaign in motion; the seagull button, an inspiration of Hennessey, was got in thousand lots, and the Railroad Audit Co. gathered material on subversive un-American

activities in the marine industry. Caucuses were held, the Mariners' Club was opened, and members were recruited and the *Rank and File Pilot* was issued on the waterfront and mailed to shipowners lists, and members of Congress, the Dies Committee and others.

Lemmon was contact man to incorporate the steamship owners and put the club on a permanent basis and to get rid of the opposition on ships, by getting them fired and to see that the ships got *Rank and File Pilots.* Washington was contacted through J. King to allow the *Rank and File Pilot* through the mails on account of irregularities in publishing the *Rank and File Pilot.*

The port-wide sit down strike was sabotaged by leaflets aboard the ships.

Steady caucuses were held nearly every day in the Commodore Hotel to break the morale of the NMU men down, start rumors and disrupt meetings and break them up, get everybody disgusted and dissatisfied. Expert advice was given by professionals of the Railroad Audit Co. Agency. The raid on the fifth floor offices was planned there and ten cent baseball bats were brought for that purpose. Everything was to be taken over and only the seagulls were to hold office, but everybody had money so naturally they bought booze and started action too early.

The issue of the balloting committee was brought up on the floor at a packed meeting with instructions who to elect; if not, to eliminate those elected. And as Ed Burke was the only objection, they decided to let him stay for appearance's sake and to sabotage the count on him. The answer is in the recount of the ballots.

Frank Steglick never joined the NMU but carries a full NMU book that is as phoney as he is a double-crosser, one of the steering committee of the Mariners' Club.

(signed) Walter Carney.

Here is Carney's *third* letter:

When O'Donohue of Houston came last year on the Sinclair Oil beef from the Gulf, the caucus of the *Rank and File* staff, J. King, Lemmon, Hennessey, Carlucci, Gallagher, Steglick and others got together on the question of the Gulf to start a Mariner's Club—methods of contacts to offset anything the membership at headquarters had done or might do, system of communication and the question of Arthur Thomas' citizenship.

Thomas was a British subject until he received a month's furlough from the membership on account of illness after the National Council meeting and returned a full citizen.

Naturalized of year's standing, this little trick was accomplished of course with the steamship owners and United Fruit Co. J. King contacted Ed Neary, Port Captain of United Fruit Co. who contacted his boss Robinson, President, and the way was paved with the help of government officials.

A. Thomas sailed on a foreign United Fruit ship on the way back with his stop off at Havana, Cuba. The British Consul had his papers all set. Upon arrival in New York he went to Washington, D. C.

With the help of the Maritime Commission the government records were falsified to show he came legally in the country years ago, so naturally he was under obligation to the United Fruit Company and the Maritime Commission. Government records at port of entry and ship will prove government and company falsifying of record and the back dating of same.

Walter Carney.

The *fourth* letter of Carney:

Through the medium of Hennessey's so-called gift of writing and when he was assistant editor of the NMU *Pilot* in order to keep alive the feeling that was brought in the union through the *Rank and File Pilot* picture, Hennessey and J. King thought up a bright idea of fabricating Trotskyite meetings and putting the leading figures of that party at a meeting, where they were supposed to come into the NMU and disrupt the meetings and to carry on a campaign to take over the NMU.

The plan in the *Rank and File Pilot* on the so-called communists meetings was termed a success and as the red herring was done to death, so the new idea was developed to build up the Trotskyite faction in order to keep the bad feeling alive and to get those officials out who weren't controllable or who did not carry out the orders of J. King.

Hennessey was paid at the rate of ten dollars for every set of minutes he produced on the lines that J. King suggested.

One copy was sent to Arthur Thomas' home in New Orleans; and another copy to O'Donohue to be mimeographed and distributed on the ships and in the halls.

Hennessey used to be so cheap he used to use NMU stationery and naturally steal the editor's secretary stamps and charge J. King for postage.

Walter Carney.

About the Railway Audit and Inspection Company, a professional strike-breaking firm, mentioned by Carney, a writer recently had this to say:

The Railway Audit and Inspection Co. provides the most thorough strike-breaking system in the country, from spies to strike-breakers, to tear-gas bombs to Thompson machine guns. It covers its espionage work with the cloaks of "human engineering" and "educational work."

It employs the frequent device of recruiting spies from among workers on the job.

Among its clients now or in the past are: [Then he names several industrial and steamship companies.]

EFFORTS TO BREAK 1936-37 STRIKE

Joseph P. Ryan, president of the ILA, was very intimately tied up with the wrecking crew. When Ryan, during that period, appeared before the Copeland Committee in Washington, he testified regarding his efforts to break the 1936-37 strike. He said:

We got some money from the shipowners. We told them it was not our fight. Our men were working, but Curran was out with goon squads.

We went to the companies and said: "Give us money; we are going to fight them." We got the money and drove them back with bats, where they belonged. Then they called the strike off.

This revelation proved that the membership had needed finally to expel the spearhead of this conspiracy to wreck the union.

Carlucci had already been exposed through the co-operation of an official of the United Electrical, Radio and Machine Workers, who saw Carlucci's picture in the *Pilot* and recognized him as the same person who had been instrumental in attempting to break a UERMWA local. The membership was therefore all ready to take the necessary action against Jerome King, whose real name was revealed as Medeiros. He was tried and expelled.

Chapter Twenty-three

THE UNION IS SAVED

The shipowners' spies, however, were also active in the
Gulf. Shortly after King's expulsion, the Gulf members
of the National Council decided to secede from the NMU.
To pave the way, they began to publish a Gulf issue of
the *Rank and File Pilot.*

The second convention of the NMU was scheduled to
begin on the first Monday in July, 1939, in New Orleans.
Joseph Curran left a week ahead of time to make necessary preparations. Upon his arrival, several attempts
were made to attack him physically. Again the rank and
file membership had to rely upon its own resources to
drive from among their ranks those who were ready to
destroy it.

Gulf delegates began to issue their own receipts and
began to hold rump meetings in each port to obtain
support for themselves. National Organizer John Rogan
was dumped in the main office of the Gulf District in
New Orleans. He was beaten with brass knuckles and
pieces of pipe. When the membership tried to come to
Rogan's aid, they were held off with guns. Leader of
this attacking group was none other than a Gulf official
who had been elected by the membership to protect and
guard the membership.

EGGLESTON KILLED

While the convention was getting underway, the body of Robert Eggleston, bookkeeper in the New Orleans office, was found buried along the waterfront in New Orleans. The disrupters were indeed desperate and were not stopping at murder in their campaign to destroy the union.

What took place at this convention is carefully recorded in the convention minutes. During the first week, credentials were presented by two groups of delegates from the Gulf. One group consisted of those who had openly proclaimed that they were going to secede from the NMU. The other group claimed election at rank and file meetings held in the various ports in the Gulf area. The delegates at this convention who represented crews from ships, as well as delegates elected at rank and file meetings in the Lakes, Atlantic and Gulf areas, determined the validity of the respective sets of credentials. F. P. O'Donohue, one of the seceding officials who sought to be seated, was exposed as a stool pigeon and expelled.

Each of the Gulf agents was given a full opportunity to stand up before the delegates and have his say. C. H. Applewhite, William C. McCuistion, and Arthur Thomas, one after another arose and faced the delegates at the convention. And yet, in spite of this disruption, the Credentials Committee made the following report:

In regard to the Gulf shore delegates, it is the recommendation of your committee that we seat the Gulf shore delegates who were elected pursuant to the ballot issued by the suspended Gulf District Committee, and that we also seat all delegates elected properly at membership meetings, pursuant to the emergency call of the National President.

Frank Rinaldo, C. H. Applewhite, William McCuistion, and O'Donohue were unseated, however, because of their open challenge to the authority of the National Office. Applewhite, Charles DeGress, McCuistion, Rinaldo, and O'Donohue were expelled by a vote of the convention delegates. O'Donohue admitted that his name was Bridges and that he had been shipping scabs during the tanker strike.

CRAFT DIVISIONS WIPED OUT

After expelling the disrupters the convention got down to the business of amending the constitution. It was apparent that the division into three districts, with separate craft divisions in each district, carried with it the craft philosophy which was abhorrent to and irreconcilable with true industrial unionism. The delegates took steps to wipe out this division and to unify the organization.

The constitution that came out of this convention is indeed a document that deserves the praise which it has already received from students of the trade union movement and which has already proved its worth during the past seven years.

Mr. Russell Nixon, Instructor of Economics at Harvard University, after examining the constitution of NMU, stated: "The NMU Constitution is the most democratic union constitution of which I have knowledge." He also declared that he was impressed with the "real democratic spirit and the active participation of the rank and file in union meetings. NMU members seem to really value union democracy, and make the most of it." Mr. Nixon further stated:

Democracy in a labor union, as in a nation, requires officers who are responsible to their constitutents (the rank and file), courts and trial procedures which guarantee free and honest expression of membership desires, and a democratic press responsible to the will of the rank and file.

The Constitution of the National Maritime Union provides all these democratic guarantees.

Chapter Twenty-four

ATTACK FROM WITHOUT

During the spring strike, the shipowners did not take the rank and file movement too seriously. It was not until joint strike action between the East Coast and West Coast in the fall of 1936 had taken place, that the shipowners became truly alarmed. They were impelled not only to inaugurate a campaign to destroy the union from within, but also to invoke the assistance of governmental agencies and the reactionary elements in Congress as well. Curiously enough, they got their chief weapon as the result of a marine disaster.

In September, 1934, the cruise ship *Morro Castle*, owned by the Ward Line, was gutted by fire off the New Jersey coast, with a loss of 134 lives. Naturally, the company tried to blame the crew. Inspired newspaper stories, running for days after the tragedy, abounded with sly innuendoes and implications that the crew lacked discipline.

The writer was a member of the *Morro Castle* Proctor's Committee selected to represent in court the 518

claimants—including widows, orphans, and other rela-
tives of the dead.

A payment of more than three-quarters of a million
dollars was ample proof that it was the neglect of the
shipowners and not the purported lack of discipline
among the seamen that was responsible for the extraordinary loss of lives.

It developed that one of the chief reasons for loss of
life had been the lack of tools by which fire hoses were
attached to hydrants.   Nevertheless, newspaper agitation
convinced many people that the crew was to blame.   This
made it possible for Secretary of Commerce Roper to
give the shipowners a powerful weapon against the seamen.

This weapon was legal—a law giving the Bureau of
Marine Inspection and Navigation the right to inquire
into alleged "misconduct" of crews on complaints of the
operators.   It can be readily seen what this meant.   Misconduct could be anything from refusal to obey orders to
joining a union.

SAFETY LAWS TO PROTECT SEAMEN USED AGAINST SEAMEN

Thus, when the seamen began to build their own
union, the shipowners had a tailor-made, anti-labor weapon at their disposal.   This is how it worked:

In August, 1937, while the SS *California* was passing
through the Panama Canal Zone, the officers in charge
mustered out but one additional deck watch to assist the
Canal Zone crew to tie up the vessel.   One of the seamen
sustained an injury in the groin directly attributable to
the insufficient number of men mustered on deck to
handle the heavy lines.   When the time arrived to untie

the vessel and make her ready for sea, the crew demanded that all hands be called on deck for this operation. For centuries it had been the tradition and custom of the sea that all three deck watches be called out on deck during a mooring and unmooring operation, but since the company (IMM) was required to pay overtime for the work done by the men who were off duty, the shipowners elected to abandon this custom to call all hands on deck. The crew refused to untie the vessel unless the entire deck crew were turned to.

Upon the vessel's arrival in her home port, a Marine Investigating Board was convened to try the entire deck crew of the *California* for refusing to obey the officer's command. An obliging bureau suspended their certificates.

Case after case was then brought by the shipowners against members of the crews for their refusal to obey the commands of their officers, when, as a matter of fact, the incidents which provoked the filing of charges were nothing more than the legitimate exercise by these seamen of their right under the Wagner Act.

THE BUREAU'S BIAS

The NMU in a long memorandum to Secretary of Commerce Harry Hopkins reviewed all of the abuses that were perpetrated by the Bureau of Marine Inspection and Navigation. This memorandum pointed out with great detail instances of bias displayed by the Bureau of Marine Inspection and Navigation—bias in favor of shipowners and licensed officers and against the unlicensed members of the crew. Remissions of fines imposed on shipowners for violation of inspection laws were recounted and the leniency exercised in favor of licensed officers enumerated.

The following are illustrations of the special favors granted shipowners by the bureau:

In the case of the SS *Azalea City,* during July 1937, the second engineer had failed to stay on board while the vessel was in various foreign ports. As required by the statute, penalties totaling $3,500 were imposed. These penalties were reduced to $175.

The master of the SS *Gulfwax,* in July, 1937, was fined $500 for failing to divide the crew into equal watches. This penalty was reduced to $25.

A fine of $500 was imposed upon the owners of the SS *Otho* for requiring an assistant engineer to work in excess of eight hours in one day. This fine was remitted entirely on the theory that the services had been performed in expectation of overtime payment and was, therefore, voluntary in character.

Penalties aggregating $27,500 imposed upon the owners of the SS *Atlantic* for requiring officers to do work in excess of eight hours in one day were reduced to $1,100.

A fine imposed on the owners of the SS *Tampa* in the sum of $1400 was reduced by the department to $100.

In issues involving the conflicting claims of officers against seamen, in every instance favor was shown for officers as against the unlicensed personnel. Yet in spite of the recital of these prejudices, nothing was done about it.

Up to the time when the bureau's activities were transferred to the United States Coast Guard, this anti-union bias continued. Protests by the NMU and other marine unions were useless. The bureau, by investigating alleged misconduct of seamen during labor disputes, was engaged in open intimidation of workers who were exercising their legal and constitutional rights. These investigations of seamen during labor disputes constituted an exercise of authority which was even denied to the United States courts when Congress passed the Norris-LaGuardia Anti-Injunction Act.

Senator Copeland, who had introduced the continuous discharge book in 1936 and who found his brainchild repealed in the spring of 1937, immediately conceived a new method of hobbling merchant seamen.

In November, 1937, he introduced a bill to impose compulsory mediation in the industry—a bill which would virtually eliminate strikes by long drawn-out arbitration. Delays which were incidental to enforced periods of mediation are especially dangerous to newly organized unions.

Hearings were conducted by the Senate Commerce Committee. Witness after witness pointed out how utterly disastrous compulsory mediation would be for the industry. NLRB chairman J. Warren Madden, who appeared before the Copeland Committee on December 13, made the following observation:

The railroad industry had gone through long experience in these matters, and was accustomed to the rights of employees set forth in that act. This is by no means true at this time in the maritime industry or in industries generally other than the railroads; so that there would seem no reason to single out the maritime industry as one in which the procedure of the National Labor Relations Act should be supplanted in so far as unfair labor practices are concerned by the criminal process of the district court, or by definition of those unfair labor practices in any manner different from those applicable to industry generally as set forth in the National Labor Relations Act.

Secretary Frances Perkins, in a letter addressed to Congressman Bland, stated:

Compulsory arbitration is at best a device for an industry which is ready for a mature labor policy. Labor relations in shipping are still in their infancy.

Again, the militancy of the NMU and the thoroughness with which it prepared its case before the Senate Committee resulted in the defeat of this second attempt to put a dog collar this time on *all* of the merchant seamen at once.

BRADLEY'S ACCUSATIONS

In May, 1938, while the campaign in the Great Lakes was developing momentum, Congressman Fred Bradley of Michigan rose in the House of Representatives and delivered himself of a wholly reckless and unwarranted attack upon the NMU.

The utter abandon with which Congressman Bradley made one wild accusation after another aroused the suspicions of NMU officials. What was the source of such a voluble and baseless attack upon the Union? Bradley had no facts. He simply repeated without verification, the vilifications of expelled NMU officials.

The NMU, as a result of an organizing campaign in the years 1937-1938, succeeded in bringing most of the Atlantic and Gulf seamen into one industrial union. At the time Congressman Bradley spoke, the union was engaged in an aggressive campaign to organize the Great Lakes and the inland waterways. Of these things the union was proud. And it is because Congressman Bradley feared that the NMU would succeed in its campaign that he took it upon himself recklessly to undermine the prestige of the NMU.

But there is another reason why Congressman Bradley carried on his campaign against the union. Congressman Bradley happens to belong to the Bradley family, which is prominent in Great Lakes shipping and which founded the Bradley Transportation Company. Since the organization of the NMU in the Great Lakes, this steamship company had been compelled to increase wages, improve working conditions, and make vessels more seaworthy. It is not unlikely, therefore, that Congressman Bradley was motivated by his proprietary interests in the shipping industry.

This attack, of course, did not go unchallenged. The NMU immediately published a document in which it challenged Congressman Bradley's integrity. It asked why Congressman Bradley did not attack on the floor of Congress the reactionary president of the Longshoremen's Union, Joseph P. Ryan. Congressman Bradley was asked why he didn't investigate the activities of Joseph P. Ryan and his $25,000 salary, if he was interested in unions which were controlled by their officials and whose activities did not serve the membership.

Many other inquiries were made of Congressman Bradley, but he knew that the immunity enjoyed by him as a congressman did not make it necessary for him to explain his statements. His attack upon the union was a part of a congressional campaign to frustrate in every possible way organizations among the maritime workers of America.

As soon as the effect of Congressman Bradley's attack

had subsided, in January, 1941, Congressman Dirksen of Illinois introduced a bill which provided for:

1. Additional citizenship requirements for crews manning the vessels.
2. Government hiring halls.
3. Compulsory mediation in the shipping industry.

The NMU again, because of thorough preparation and documentary proof submitted at the Committee hearings, succeeded in repelling Congressman Dirksen's attack.

ATTACK BY CONGRESSMAN DIES

The growth of the trade union movement, rather than the supposedly subversive activities, was largely responsible for the creation of the Dies Committee. Was it a mere coincidence that the resolution authorizing the Dies investigation was adopted at the very time that the shipowners were engaged in a campaign to destroy marine unions from within? During the very month that balloting in the first NMU election was completed and when the campaign to destroy the union was reaching its height, Congressman Dies began to hold his hearings in Washington. It certainly is no coincidence that the NMU was one of the first unions attacked and its officials listed as Communists. For more than three days John P. Frey, president of the AFL Metal Trades Department, was permitted to testify, without interruption, and filled several hundred pages of a record which in part constituted an unrestrained attack upon the NMU. At that time the ISU, the AFL seamen's union, had been completely routed.

The whole gamut of red-baiting was indulged in by this witness. Charges that Joseph Curran, Harry Bridges, and other labor leaders were open agents of Moscow was spread on the record. Every official of the NMU was branded as a dangerous and subversive element.

In October of the following year Joseph Curran appeared before the Dies Committee and openly attacked Dies for daring to impugn his patriotism. But irreparable injury had already been done. The hearings were terminated abruptly. Congressman Dies was not taking on witnesses who fought back.

In 1939 the Dies Committee again filled several hundred pages of its record with continued attacks by expelled NMU officials like William C. McCuistion and his ilk. While McCuistion was testifying in Washington, he was arrested on a charge of murder growing out of the controversies in the Gulf. He had been indicted for the murder of Philip Carey, an official of the NMU, during the previous summer, immediately after the New Orleans convention.

Chapter Twenty-five

"DEPORT HARRY BRIDGES!"

Harry Bridges helped build a strong union of long-shoremen on the West Coast, which obtained substantial improvements for its membership. Under his leadership, the longshoremen were able to get rid of that vicious weapon of the bosses, the shape-up. As far back as 1934 Bridges had sponsored resolutions and called for action against fascism and against loading ships flying the swastika. He was also opposed to shipping scrap iron to Japan.

There were powerful people who, for these reasons, did not like Harry Bridges. They represented large money and political influences, controlled the press and the radio. These people soon enough discovered that they could not buy him and that they could not split his union from within because the members "were all for one and one for all."

Harry Bridges was born in Australia. He came to this country in 1920, but as late as 1934 he had not as yet been naturalized. Bridges' enemies seized upon these circumstances to attempt to deport him on the ground that he was a Communist. Throughout the 1934 strike and for some time thereafter, immigration authorities trailed him. In 1936, however, a memorandum was prepared by the Immigration Service exonorating him.

But the fight to get Bridges began all over again.

Philip Murray, president of the CIO, knew that the enemies of labor had been trying to "get" Bridges. Murray knew that in the files of the Department of Labor in Washington there was a memorandum prepared by three high officials of the government, which explained the forces eager to deport Bridges. The memorandum written in 1936 stated that Bridges' "deportation was then and later urgently sought by the interests which he had antagonized."

DEPORTATION PROCEEDINGS

In 1938 his enemies thought they had enough proof against him and accordingly a warrant for his arrest and deportation was issued. He was charged with being affiliated with the American Communist Party and with being sympathetic to and thereafter affiliated with the Marine Workers Industrial Union. At the protracted hearing before Dean James M. Landis of Harvard, in 1938, Bridges freely admitted that his relationship with the MWIU had always been friendly. He also stated, as his opinion, that it was largely the pressure of the MWIU that had forced the ISU officially to join the strike on May 15, 1934.

Dean Landis, after hearing 32 witnesses over a period of eleven weeks, exonerated Bridges from the charges of membership in the Communist Party. This decision resulted in a barrage of resolutions in Congress. One in 1939 was to impeach Secretary of Labor Frances Perkins for refusing to deport him. In 1940 a bill was introduced to deport Bridges. This bill was declared unconstitutional by the Attorney General because, by naming him, it constituted a bill of attainder.

Finally, since Dean Landis had held that Bridges was

not a member of the Communist Party at the time of the hearing, and the U. S. Supreme Court had held in the Strecker case that deportation could be ordered only because of *present* and not past membership, Bridges' enemies proceeded to amend the existing law. In 1940 the immigration laws were amended to make *past* membership a ground for deportation.

NEW ATTEMPT

Immediately on its passage, new deportation proceedings were brought against Bridges. Former Judge Charles B. Sears of the New York Court of Appeals was designated to preside. There was proof of illegal wire-tapping by the government to secure evidence against Bridges. Bridges again admitted that during the 1934 strike his union had accepted aid from the MWIU. He also testified that without MWIU help the longshoremen would have lost the strike.

Prior to the opening of the hearings before Judge Sears, President Philip Murray of the CIO warned:

There are individuals and groups in our nation who have been and are continuing to be primarily intent upon destroying labor organizations. These individuals and groups seek to undermine American democracy by opposing the right of workers to organize, and will do so in times of stress under the guise of patriotism. One of the most frequent attacks practiced by these enemies of labor is the one directed against the leaders of labor organizations.

Judge Sears, as was expected, ruled that Bridges should be deported. The MWIU was a subsidiary of the Trade Union Unity League. By accepting help from the MWIU, Sears held, Bridges was either a member of, or affiliated with, the Communist Party and therefore deportable.

Bridges, however, appealed to the Board of Immigration Appeals and Judge Sears' decision was reversed.

But the last card had not been played. Attorney General Francis Biddle reversed the Appeals Board, thus reinstating Judge Sears' order of deportation.

DEFIES PRECEDENT

In making this decision, Biddle not only rejected a decision of his own Appeals Board, but also upset a ruling of a solicitor general issued seven years earlier.

As far back as January, 1934, Solicitor General Charles E. Wyzanski had held that membership in the National Miners Union, the MWIU, the Trade Union Unity League, or other left wing labor unions, was not ground for deportation. His opinion, in part, stated:

For the United States to deport a man merely for membership in such a union is to deport a man for seeking to overthrow conservative union domination, not for seeking to overthrow the Government of the United States.

The United States Supreme Court finally, in 1945, held that Bridges had received "an unfair hearing on the question of his membership in the Communist Party" and that his detention under warrant was found to be unlawful. He was, thereupon, released.

Bridges has since become a citizen of the United States, but his ten-year struggle shows what powerful forces can be set into motion to destroy a valiant fighter in the struggle to better the workers' conditions.

It is important to note here that had the fight against the deportation of Bridges been limited to the courts, there is no doubt in the writer's mind that the shipowners would have succeeded. It was the mass fight which was conducted by maritime workers and the rest of the American labor movement, in the form of protests, resolutions, mass meetings, and financial support which secured the victory.

Chapter Twenty-six

ATTACK THROUGH THE COURTS

Not only did the organization of the NMU inspire congressmen and government officials to try and check the progress that maritime workers were making in organizing unions of their own choosing, but the shipowners invoked the assistance of the courts as well.

SS TEXAN

In June, 1934, the crew of the *SS Texan* struck while lying alongside a dock in the port of New York. This vessel was struck by the crew to secure the same conditions for which the crews on the West Coast were then striking. The crew demanded of the master that he recognize the MWIU as its collective bargaining representative, and that he grant certain demands with respect to wages and working conditions. The ISU officials on the East Coast refused to support the West Coast strikers even though on the West Coast the ISU crews were on a strike which had been officially called by the ISU officials. The striking crew was removed from the vessel and a new one was supplied by the ISU officials. The new crew was sent on board the *Texan* through a picket line established by the striking crew.

In an action brought in the Federal Court to recover the wages of the dismissed *Texan* crew, the steamship owners pleaded as a defense that the crew had forfeited their wages because, in effect, they were guilty of violating the mutiny statutes, passed in 1790. The Circuit Court rejected this plea of mutiny and awarded a judgment in favor of the crew, and the United States Supreme Court refused to entertain an appeal by the shipowners from the Circuit Court's decision.

SS CALIFORNIA

In March, 1936, the crew of the SS *California* was accused of being mutinous, and the Secretary of Commerce urged the crew be prosecuted under the mutiny statutes.

The mutiny statutes were not invoked against the crew of the SS *California* because at that time undoubtedly the shipowners were fearful of the mood of the workers and did not wish to provoke the outbreak of the suppressed storm against the miserable wages and conditions which were seething among the seamen.

SS ALGIC

In September, 1937, the crew of the SS *Algic,* while the vessel was lying at anchor in the port of Montevideo, Uruguay, refused to furnish steam to the scab longshoremen who were engaged in unloading the vessel. The longshoremen in Montevideo were on strike and scab longshoremen had been brought on board the vessel. It was not long before the crew discovered that the scabs were not skilled enough to operate the machinery, making it dangerous to be on deck. Because of this danger, the crew refused to perform its work.

The master of the vessel communicated with the Maritime Commission in Washington. When the crew was advised that the master had been given orders to dismiss them if they refused to perform their duties, they went back to work. Upon the return of the ship to this country, a national campaign was set in motion to convict the crew of mutiny.

It would be difficult to portray the anti-union sentiment that was inspired by the weird newspaper stories. The crew of the *SS Algic* was convicted. The Circuit Court, in sustaining the conviction, left open the question of whether or not they would have sustained the conviction had it been established by the seamen at the trial that the port of Montevideo had been a safe port. For that reason, no appeal was taken to the United States Supreme Court.

SS SAGE BRUSH

The extent to which the mutiny statutes were being used to intimidate merchant seamen is shown by the fact that during a strike on board the *SS Sage Brush* in Philadelphia the United States Attorney obtained an indictment against the crew under the mutiny statutes. On the petition of the NMU the indictment was squashed and the crew of the *SS Sage Brush* was not tried under the mutiny statutes.

SS CITY OF FORT WORTH

In August, 1937, the crew of the *SS City of Fort Worth* struck because the employer refused to negotiate with the

NMU. The crew repaired to the poop deck of the vessel while the master communicated with the owners of the vessel in Philadelphia. After a promise that negotiations would be conducted in good faith, the crew returned to their stations. Upon the vessel's return to Philadelphia, the crew was discharged. The NLRB, after extensive hearings were had, ruled that the discharge of the crew was an unfair labor practice, and as such violated the National Labor Relations Act. Members of the crew were ordered reinstated *with back pay*.

The company appealed to the Circuit Court of Appeals, arguing that the crew was guilty of mutiny. The United States Circuit Court of Appeals rejected the plea of the Southern Steamship Company. As a matter of fact the court held as follows:

It is, therefore, clear that upon authority the question of the right of seamen to strike under the circumstances of the case before us is still an open one. Upon reason, however, we think that there is no sound basis for depriving seamen of this right when, as here, their vessel is moored to the dock in a safe domestic port. Whether the right exists in a foreign port we need not now decide.

The United States Supreme Court granted leave to the shipowners to appeal their case. The U. S. Supreme Court reversed the Circuit Court of Appeals and in effect held that the conduct of the crew of the *SS City of Fort Worth* was mutinous, even though the vessel was moored to a dock in a safe United States port.

The implications of this decision are clear: If Congress does not make inapplicable the mutiny statutes regarding disobedience of crews to their masters' orders while a vessel is lying in a safe harbor, then merchant seamen are forever barred from benefits of the National Labor Relations Act and are made outcasts in the realm of labor relations.

The Supreme Court, although it recognized that the Circuit Court had made its decision in the belief that disobedience on a vessel moored to a dock in a safe port did not violate the statutes, still felt obliged strictly to apply the language of the statute, even though that statute was passed as far back as 1790. The only remedy available to the seamen, the Supreme Court held, was to apply to Congress for an amendment of the law affecting mutiny.

Chapter Twenty-seven

SEAMEN–EARLY ANTI-FASCISTS

Progressive workers in the maritime industry, even before the maritime strike of 1934, already realized the menace of fascism to all liberty-loving people, particularly workers. In February, 1934, a conference of rank and file longshoremen was held in San Francisco to force recognition by the ILA international officers of the new leadership headed by Harry Bridges. Among the resolutions adopted at this convention was one against the loading of ships flying the Nazi flag. Hitler had not been in power for even a year and already the far-seeing maritime workers realized that a struggle had to be carried on against the country which nurtured such a threat to democracy and to the working class in particular.

On July 5, 1935, Lawrence B. Simpson, a member of the ISU, was forcibly removed from the *SS Manhattan* by Nazi government agents while the ship was enroute from Cuxhaven to Hamburg. He was removed from the vessel by Nazi police, ostensibly for having anti-Nazi literature in his locker.

Rank and file seamen immediately protested this unwarranted interference with their rights. The ship's officers did nothing to prevent this outrageous violation of their rights, nor did the American Consul at Hamburg for a while do anything to ascertain the cause for Simpson's arrest. The rank and file seamen immediately began a campaign for his release.

The literature in Simpson's locker may have been no more than a newspaper or magazine article in which the Nazi atrocities were being criticized. Under the German laws of that period, any literature which in any way impugned the integrity of the Third Reich or the Fuehrer would have been sufficient to cause the arrest of its possessor. To have singled out an unlicensed merchant seaman for arrest because he possessed literature which criticized the Nazi government could not be interpreted as anything but an attack upon the rights of American merchant seamen—an attack upon the ordinary rights of an American citizen in the exercise of his constitutional rights while employed on an American vessel. A national campaign for Simpson's release was begun by the rank and file seamen in the ISU. Simpson was ultimately released.

PROTESTED FASCIST CARGOES

The intensity of the campaign on the part of the American merchant seamen, which ultimately resulted in Simpson's release, was an indication of the strong feeling of merchant seamen on fascism.

As far back as October, 1935, the Portland, Oregon Central Labor Council had voted a ban on cargo destined for fascist Italy. A report submitted by one of the delegates at the council warned that should Italian ships venture into Portland, they would probably lie in the river a long time before they would find longshoremen to handle cargo on Italian boats destined for fascist countries.

During the latter part of November, 1935, the maritime workers in San Pedro, California, refused to permit the *SS Oregon,* an American vessel, and the *SS Rignor,* a Norwegian vessel, to load oil and gasoline which was destined for Mussolini's fascist army. The ships were picketed and the longshoremen were determined that this murder cargo would stay where it was and not be moved where it could destroy innocent Ethiopians.

During the same month, the British ship *Farnham* was struck in the port of Boston: It refused to carry scrap steel which was destined for Mussolini's munitions factories. This determination on the part of the maritime workers to prevent death cargoes to be transported to the fascist countries impelled some members of the President's cabinet to make public statements on the matter. The *Times* of November 25 stated:

Secretary of Labor Frances Perkins gave encouragement today to workers who are refusing to load cargoes or man ships carrying supplies destined for Italy.

Aligning herself with Interior Secretary Harold L. Ickes

and other officials who previously have given approval to various aspects of the administration's neutrality policy in the African War, she expressed confidence at a press conference that arbitrators would support, as in line with the government's views, the stand of union laborers who struck against manning ships carrying materials to the belligerents.

The laborers, of course, she explained, should refer their cases to arbitrators in the various ports for final decision.

THE WAR IN SPAIN

In February, 1936, a people's government was swept into office in Spain. The people of Spain rebelled against serfdom; they craved freedom of speech and they hoped that the right to join trade unions would be theirs. The fascists of the world, however, had planned otherwise, and it was not long after these elections that the entire country was overrun with fascists and their murderous weapons. Many of the seamen who were on strike on the American waterfront were Spaniards. Almost all the seamen had at one time or another worked with Spanish seamen, and a great many of them were employed on ships that occasionally docked in Spain.

As the war progressed and the participation of fascist Italy and Nazi Germany became clear, many American workers decided to do what they could to enter that country and fight for its freedom. Merchant seamen were among those workers. It was a long time before the liberty-loving people throughout the world saw that the fight of Spanish democracy against world fascism was their fight. It took the democratic peoples many years to realize that in Spain were being fought the preliminary battles of World War II.

Yes, many seamen left the picket line—some even before the strike was over—to fight in Spain. More than a thousand merchant seamen fought in that war. Many are buried in Spain. The Abraham Lincoln Brigade, among which were scores of merchant seamen, covered itself with glory. After their return, the Spanish defenders rejoined the ranks of their fellow trade unionists to continue the struggle to improve the working conditions in their respective industries.

Chapter Twenty-eight

THE ROLE OF MERCHANT SEAMEN IN WORLD WAR II

Long before Pearl Harbor, merchant seamen had been coming up against the ugly face of fascism. American ships were entering German, Italian, and Spanish ports. The imprisonment of Lawrence Simpson and their participation on the side of the Loyalists in the Spanish Civil War gave the merchant seamen a real taste of fascism.

World War II broke out in September, 1939. The New Orleans convention which almost wrecked the union had terminated only a month before. Between the commencement of hostilities and Pearl Harbor, the application of the Neutrality Act excluded many ships from European waters. During the early days of the war, there was general dissatisfaction among American seamen with the manner in which the war was fought. At some stages it did not appear to be fought as a people's war, as a war to defeat fascism. Feeling that way about it, the seamen were outspoken.

When attacked by rabid publicists, they fought back. Walter Winchell, in a broadcast one Sunday and in the *Daily Mirror* of June of 1941, attacked the NMU members, questioning their loyalty. The union fought right back with a law-suit and made history by compelling both Winchell and his sponsors to pay almost $20,000 damages for his libelous statement.

When the union's opposition to the manner in which the war was carried on was later under attack, President Curran pointed out that the union's fight against fascism began long before the outbreak of World War II. It began in 1935 over the issue of shipping scrap iron to Japan, the deliberate refusal of Britain, France, and the United States to assist the Loyalists in Spain, and their joining in refusing to assist Haile Selassie in his plea before the League of Nations when fascism could have been smashed.

At the union's Third Convention, held in Cleveland almost six months before Pearl Harbor, the imminent struggle with fascism was thoroughly discussed. Towards its close it was enunciated that the union was vitally concerned with defense. In his closing statement, President Curran declared:

National defense means much to us. We love our country far more than those who wave the flag and make patriotic speeches. We work at defending our country. We work at defending our union. We work at defending the democratic institutions of this country and we are attempting to expand those things, for we believe this is real national defense.

"WE'LL KEEP 'EM SAILING"

Two days after Pearl Harbor, recognizing the vital role which the merchant marine would play in the war, the union wired Chairman Emory S. Land of the United States Maritime Commission of its readiness to join with government and industry in formulating a constructive policy.

At a conference held in Washington, December 17, 1941, the NMU came forward with concrete proposals:

1. The arming of all merchant vessels.
2. Increase in the manning scale.
3. Proper inspection and servicing of life boats.
4. More efficient training program in Maritime Commission Schools.
5. Training of seamen in gunnery and first aid.
6. Maintenance of collective bargaining contracts.
7. Adequate check-up of personnel.
8. Proper handling of foreign seamen's questions.

The slogan of "We'll Keep 'Em Sailing" became the creed of every American seaman.

When the torpedoing and collisions began to take their enormous toll of ship's personnel, a campaign of "safety" was inaugurated. Better loading of ships was urged upon shoreside maritime workers.

To preserve life and morale of the seamen, proper provisioning of life boats, the establishment of safety committees on each ship, and the proper training of new personnel was fought for.

Upgrading schools and model ship's equipment were established at the NMU Hall. Seamen surviving the scores of torpedoings appeared before the public. They told their stories to bring home the horrors of war and the enormity of the tasks ahead.

HEROES IN DUNGAREES

The valor of merchant seamen during the early days of the war when as many as eight ships were torpedoed in one day impelled reference to them as "Heroes in Dungarees."

Nick Hoogendam, a seventeen-year old member of the NMU, together with his two companions was rescued after spending 83 days on an open raft. No log in maritime history has ever disclosed a saga of such stamina, courage, and desire to live to continue to fight for freedom.

On October 8, 1942, President Roosevelt pinned the first Merchant Marine Distinguished Service Medal on the breast of Edwin F. Cheney, Jr., a member of the National Maritime Union. This is what the President said:

For heroism above and beyond the call of duty during enemy attack when he released and launched a life raft from a sinking and burning ship and maneuvered it through a pool of burning oil to clear water by swimming underwater, coming up only to breathe. Although he had incurred severe burns about the face and arms in this action, he then guided four of his shipmates to the raft and swam to and rescued two others who were injured and unable to help themselves.

His extraordinary courage and disregard of his own safety in thus rescuing his shipmates will be an enduring inspiration to seamen of the United States Merchant Marine everywhere.

Seaman Cheney's acts of heroism were repeated a hundredfold. And despite all these hardships, the war cargoes kept moving.

NMU FIGHTS DISCRIMINATION

Fighting discrimination was nothing new for the NMU. The first article of the first constitution stated that one of the objectives of the union was "to unite in our organization, regardless of creed, color, nationality or political affiliation, all workers eligible for membership directly or indirectly engaged in maritime industry."

In the opening paragraphs of the pamphlet issued by the Union entitled *The NMU Fights Jim Crow* we find reference made to the observation of Karl Marx that "Labor cannot emancipate itself in the white skin where in the black it is branded."

The NMU fought for racial equality by practicing it and proving that it was not only possible but a positive good.

In June, 1942, the luxury liner *Kungsholm* was taken over by the United States Lines. A crew of 140 was asked for and dispatched to the ship. One hundred fifteen were accepted; the cards of 25 were marked "not acceptable." They were Negroes. A protest to Washington resulted in the shipping of all 25 previously rejected.

A series of such incidents convinced the shipowners that Jim Crowism would not be tolerated. In September of 1942, because of pressure from the NMU members on ships all over the world, Captain Hugh Mulzac was appointed to command the new Liberty freighter, *Booker T. Washington*. Captain Mulzac was the first Negro ever to command a merchant vessel.

ENEMIES WITHIN STRIKE AT NMU

The members and officials of the union participated in the political life of the country throughout the war.

In August, 1942, often referred to as "the period of the crisis," the National Maritime Union released a letter to "Mr. and Mrs. America, U.S.A." from "The Men Who Sail Your Ships." This document urged the opening of a second front. Since the end of the war, the practicability and desirability of opening up a second front in 1942 had been established. To the enemy at home this demand was heresy. This and similar demands inspired many attacks upon the union. The vilest of all these attacks was the one carried in *The Akron Beacon Journal* which was picked up by the A.P. and appeared in every hamlet newspaper throughout the land.

On January 21, 1943 that paper carried the streamer, "Ship 'Strike' Ires Guadalcanal Fighters." The story purported to deal with a refusal of a crew to unload cargo on Sunday. This story inspired headlines such as "Order Probe of CIO Scandal in Guadalcanal." "Marines Unload on CIO Holiday." "Reds in Control Over Crews of American Ships." "House Inquiry Begun into CIO Pacific Scandal."

These headlines clearly show that this concocted attack was directed more against labor and the CIO in particular than against the seamen. The anti-labor forces in America were testing their ground.

Only the most reckless newspapers carried the story. The House inquiry revealed the story as spurious. Admiral Halsey and others of similar rank repudiated it. The NMU began four actions for damages in four different cities.

The Colonel of the Marines in charge of the unloading of cargo on the two-mile beachhead at Guadalcanal has since testified under oath. He put the lie to the story by stating that the merchant crews could not get out of

Guadalcanal fast enough because of the terrific strafing from dive bombers. The court actions have, as yet, not been tried.

Clearly, these attacks had no effect on the spirit or valor of the merchant seamen. They delivered men and ships to North Africa, to Sicily, to Italy, to Murmansk, to every island in the Pacific. Proportionally, more merchant seamen lost their lives in the merchant marine than in any other branch of the armed services. There are no white crosses standing over the graves but their kin remember and bear a heavier burden because they are gone.

FIGHT TO BRING BACK THE GI'S

After V. J. Day the task of bringing back the fighting men posed itself as a new problem. Why the soldiers were not being returned as fast as they might have been could not be explained. Many reasons were given, among them that ships were not available. Well, the seamen knew whether ships were or were not available. They knew that some of the cargoes were not quite essential. They knew that ships were being misused and that the ships could be found to bring the boys home.

President Curran went on the air on November 27, 1945, on a coast to coast hook-up. He spoke to the wives, sweethearts, and families of the GI's, told them why the GI's were snafu'd. He also promised that every ship would be examined and reports made of ships that could be made available.

President Philip Murray, in an address to the American Legion Convention that month, demanded "the fast return of our troops from abroad."

The NMU then announced that December 23, 1945,

was set as a 24 hour ship stoppage in every port in the land. All maritime unions including longshoremen participated in the work stoppage. The response was 100 per cent. All the GI's all over the world felt the solidarity of this action. Marching seamen were seen by the American people in every city where a ship was tied up.

This stoppage was trade unionism in action. It reverberated throughout the land.

Chapter Twenty-nine

THE FIGHT FOR PORK CHOPS SINCE V.E. DAY

The attacks upon the CIO in general and the merchant seamen in particular were not restricted to base charges of the kind resorted to in the Guadalcanal strike story. The majority of the unions engaged in war work were CIO unions. Steel, auto, rubber, aluminum, shipbuilding and shipping in particular were singled out for attack.

THE MYTH OF HIGH WAGES

The Hearst and Scripps-Howard chains began their attacks on the "high wages" that were being paid to merchant seamen. The device resorted to by these papers to prove that merchant seamen are literally rolling in wealth was to compare the wages paid to the *lowest* paid navyman with the *highest* paid merchantman.

The progressive newspaper *PM* in New York exposed this trick. By consulting the United States Maritime Service and the official figures of government payrolls in the Navy, they were able to expose the fraud. The truth was that (1) Petty officer's income after tax in the Navy was $2,308.68; (2) Able seamen's income after tax in the Merchant Marine was $2,163.58. Clearly the navyman was $145.10 ahead of the merchantman.

Similarly, if killed, dependents of a navyman received an annuity of $11,500; whereas a merchantman's dependents received $5,000 as a flat sum.

Other illustrations were given showing the advantages enjoyed by navy personnel over merchantmen.

The "high" wages received by seamen actually were not paid as wages. Wages, as such, were fixed at $100 for AB's. Then a 100 per cent steaming bonus was added while the vessel was under way. Area bonuses and attack bonuses were also added when conditions required it. The total received by a merchant seaman actually included as much money representing compensation for *risks* as for work performed.

At different times, officials of the NMU served as labor representatives in government agencies organized to further the war effort. They served on such agencies as the United Seamen's Service, an organization that performed heroic service for disabled seamen as well as the needs of their families while they were at sea; the War Shipping Panel, established to resolve labor disputes; the Maritime Council, organized to further the contribution of the American Merchant Marine to the successful fulfillment of its tasks, and other agencies of less importance.

POLITICS IS OUR BREAD AND BUTTER

Oldtimers began to say that "lately the union is going in too much for political affairs. It is losing its militancy because of going into politics."

The officials of the Union, who knew exactly how the oldtimers felt and thought, but who met the shipowners regularly during negotiations, knew how helpful politics could be to increase the pork chops. The theme of a pamphlet issued by the union, entitled *Pork Chops and Politics* is expressed in the following few sentences:

We have no choice in the matter. The fight on the picket line is not enough—we must go to politics.

Politics, to be perfectly frank and simple about it, is our bread and butter.

It was pointed out that :

The Copeland fink book was licked because of politics.

The Dirksen Bill which attempted to impose compulsory mediation on the marine industry was licked because of politics.

Attempts of the shipowners to put seamen under a compensation act and deprive them of the Jones Act and the General Admiralty laws' protection was licked because of political action. Joseph Curran and Harry Lundeberg both appeared before a Senate Committee. All of the Columbia professors that the shipowners brought down didn't help.

It was also trade union participation in politics which helped re-elect President Franklin Delano Roosevelt.

All seamen cannot vote because of restrictive registration laws of the various states but they can ring doorbells real hard.

Seamen may not be able to cast a ballot in the box but they can act as watchers at the polls.

Nationally, in 1944, the CIO showed the workers of America the value of political action. For fifty years the AFL shunned politics, but in 1944 the CIO had its National Political Action Committee.

During the 1944 presidential campaign, the NMU issued a pamphlet giving instructions on how to organize political action aboard a ship as well as how to participate while in port. Families were urged by letters to take more interest in politics and while in port seamen rang doorbells, urged neighbors to register, distributed literature, and helped organize meetings.

President Roosevelt was re-elected in 1944 by the labor vote and workers above all should never forget that.

FIGHTING FOR "REAL" WAGES

As the war was drawing to a close, the National Council of the union did prepare a Post-War Shipping Program but no sooner was the fighting over in Europe than wage cuts for seamen were ordered.

During the war, the Maritime War Emergency Board had jurisdiction over the payment of bonus for risks and hazards to which seamen were exposed. War risk insurance was also supervised by this agency.

Wartime take-home pay of seamen, as has already been indicated, consisted of the base pay plus bonuses.

After V.E. Day seamen's wages were the easiest to attack. On July 15, 1945, the MWEB ordered that bonuses be cut, because risks in European waters had terminated. This reduction amounted to a wage slash of almost 50 per cent. Computed on an hourly basis, the American seamen, following the cut, was receiving a base pay of 34½ cents an hour.

The NMU then presented its case to the National War Labor Board which had jurisdiction over all wages nationally. The NWLB had fixed 55 cents an hour as the minimum wage to be paid to workers. The board declared that any wage rate below that was a substandard wage rate.

During the war, the NWLB had guided itself by what what was known as the Little Steel Formula—this formula prohibited the granting of wage increases of more than 15 per cent above the base pay received by a worker on the first day of January, 1941. To grant an increase from 34½ cents an hour to 55 cents an hour would clearly be a violation of the Little Steel Formula.

The NMU jointly with other maritime unions in their case before the NWLB exposed the strategy of the shipowners in labeling wartime wage increases as war bonuses; that if bonuses were recognized for what they really were, the increase to 55 cents an hour would be permissible.

A nationwide campaign was launched to raise the seamen's wages at least to that level, below which it would be a substandard wage rate. Some radio commentators were moved to action and publicity of the most energetic kind was set in motion.

The NWLB by its decision, dated October 31, 1945 (17 L.R.R.1515), awarded an increase of $45.00 per month in the base rate of all classifications to take effect when the current voyage bonus was eliminated.

Chapter Thirty

UNITE–OR BE SMASHED

The record of struggle of merchant seamen narrated in these pages reveals the conflict between industry and labor in its rawest state. The LaFollette investigation in 1937 exposed few incidents that were more brutal.

For the American seamen, because of the status they held under the law prior to 1915, these struggles sought to achieve their proper status in the economic, political and social life of the nation. Release from economic bondage was their goal and in 1947 it is fair to assume that they moved a considerable distance towards its attainment.

Ultimate success can, however, be won if greater unity is attained for the struggles that are looming up. If seamen are to learn anything it is that the solutions of their problems depend upon the establishment of more effective and complete unity of organization, purpose, and action.

In 1921, it is true, there was what appeared to be a single union in the field. The ISU in reality was a confederation of almost twenty independent and autonomous unions. Each union had its own set of officers, its own treasury and members employed in one craft. In addition to being divided into crafts the unions were grouped into three districts: Atlantic and Gulf, Pacific, and Great Lakes.

Other marine unions of longshoremen and licensed officers were directly affiliated with the American Federation of Labor. Nevertheless, in 1919, during the longshoremen's strike, offshore unions refused to help, and in 1921 the longshoremen responded in kind. Disunity was the major cause for the disastrous strike of 1921.

Between 1930 and 1934 the Marine Workers Industrial Union made an effort to unite in one organization all crafts on each ship as well as longshoremen and inland boatmen. When the West Coast 1934 longshore strike first began, the MWIU immediately organized the support of seagoing workers for the longshoremen. So effective was this support of the MWIU that, as has already been shown, the ISU officials were forced to join the West Coast strikers. The ISU officials gave their support most reluctantly, actually to save their union from dissolution. On the East Coast no support was given by the ISU to the strikers in 1934. Harry Bridges was the first to recognize the role played by the MWIU in the 1934 West Coast strike.

SHIPOWNERS CONNIVE AGAINST UNITY

During the spring and summer of 1934, the same unity did not exist on the East Coast. In the winter of that year, the East Coast shipowners, hoping to prevent such unity, quickly signed an agreement with the ISU officials on the East Coast.

The MWIU, in the winter of 1934, recognized that unity could only be achieved by a merger of the ISU and the MWIU. An offer to merge was made. This idea was rejected by the ISU officials, and the MWIU dissolved its organization and the memberships merged their strength in the ISU. This unity achieved two things: (1)

the expulsion and elimination of the corrupt officials, and (2) the organization of the NMU.

The first convention of the NMU made a heroic effort to eliminate all craft and sectional divisions but, because of the tradition in the industry, this could not be accomplished at the first convention. The failure to achieve this unity almost wrecked this young union.

In the summer of 1939, after the spies in the NMU had been exposed, a final attempt was made to smash the union.

The Gulf District demanded autonomy. Gulf officials began to publish their own newspaper, *The Gulf Pilot,* and to act as a separate union. The membership defeated this separatist movement and the New Orleans convention revised the constitution in the direction of firmer unity. It was clear that the call for autonomy by the Gulf District was a last call for disunity.

ISU DISAPPEARS

The overwhelming victory of the NMU over the ISU in the 1937-38 Labor Board elections established, for a while, one union in the industry. So complete was the rout of the ISU that it finally disappeared altogether.

The shipowners, however, could not afford this growing unity of the maritime workers. When the planting of labor spies in the NMU failed to smash this union, they felt it was necessary to build a rival union. Seafarers International Union suddenly came into the picture.

The shipowners, at first, began to give direct assistance to this union during labor board elections. The Waterman case is an example.

The Waterman Steamship Company actually dismissed the NMU crews of the *SS Bienville* and the *SS Fairland.*

After long-drawn-out proceedings before the NLRB, finally ending in the United States Supreme Court, the company was forced to offer to reinstate the NMU crews with back pay. But the pattern for collaboration between the SIU and the shipowners was set.

The Waterman Steamship Company persisted in its collaboration with the newly organized Seafarers International Union (AFL). It offered contracts with provisions even better than those contained in NMU contracts.

This steamship company took the lead in helping to build a strong rival to the NMU. The perspective for the shipowners was to have two rival unions of almost equal strength in the field and use one against the other to drive down conditions.

The shipowners have one objective, that is, weaken the unions by internal differences and external rivalries. Rank and file seamen of all unions, whether CIO or AFL or unaffiliated, must realize one thing: The struggle is close at hand.

FURTHER ATTEMPTS AT UNITY

Soon after the NMU became affiliated with the CIO in July, 1937, President John L. Lewis called a conference to bring about unity between the maritime unions. The first convened in Lewis' office with a view to establishing the basis for national unity. Delegates from all the maritime unions came with the exception of the SIU.

During the year 1937, the NLRB has ordered elections, and although another unity conference was called for September, 1937, in Chicago, little progress was made.

The Maritime Federation of the Pacific struggled for unity but with the new struggle for industrial organization, the component unions soon realized that the form of organization which the Federation took was outmoded in 1937. The Federation was a federated group of craft unions and although it provided a powerful instrument and weapon for the seamen in the early AFL days, with the coming of a new era and a higher and stronger form of trade unionism, industrial unionism, the Federation had become an impediment. The Federation was dissolved.

Conditions in the NMU between 1938 and 1941 were such that organic unity with other member unions was not possible. At the 1941 convention of the NMU in Cleveland, the first substantial and serious attempt to bring about unity between the majority of the maritime unions took place. The West Coast unions sent twenty-six delegates to this convention. The American Communications Association was represented by three.

The convention appointed a unity committee of 58— twenty-nine NMU members to meet with 29 from the outside unions. The unions represented, besides the NMU, were the MCS Association of the Pacific, the MFOW of the Pacific, the ACA and the Inland Boatmen's Union of the Pacific.

The MCS of the Pacific held a referendum vote and the unity vote was rejected. The MFOW never took one. After this failure, no attempts at unity were undertaken. During the war period little thought was given to it. But after V.J. Day much thinking was done.

COMMITTEE FOR MARITIME UNITY

In February, 1946, after many months of stalling by the shipowners during contract negotiations that had begun shortly after V.J. Day, seven maritime unions met in Washington to discuss their common problems.

The report of the conference, attended by the ACA,

IBU, ILWU, MEBA, MFOW, MCS and NMU, high-
lighted the need of "one national union for maritime
workers." The national union, it was agreed, should:

1. Be empowered to co-ordinate strike action affecting
more than one organization.
2. Endeavor to promote national uniform agreements.
3. Be responsible to assure the full organization of the
unorganized in the industry.
4. Establish a national research department.
5. Direct national political action.
6. Publish an official national organ.

A convention was called for May 6, 1946, at San Francisco. By the time the delegates met, it was clear that
strike action would be unavoidable.

The statement of policy on joint strike action issued
by the San Francisco convention declared in part as follows:

To the extent possible and practical the unions shall conduct joint negotiations with the shipowners. In view of the
foregoing we resolve that the national strike action against
the shipping industry shall be joint action with all maritime
unions concerned starting the strike together on June 15,
1946 at 12:01 A.M., local time, and continuing to remain on
strike until the demands of all the respective unions are met.

Joint negotiations were conducted in Washington until the deadline of midnight of June 15. Preparations for
a strike were so thorough that the whole country had become aware of the seriousness of the situation. A settlement was reached and the strike was averted.

CMU GAINS

The Committee for Maritime Unity broke through
the 56-hour week at sea for the first time in the history of

the maritime industry. The 48-hour week was established with Sunday as an overtime day. Those gains won by
the CMU became standard even for unorganized seamen
and for the groups whose contracts were not open, such
as the Masters, Mates and Pilots, AFL.

During the negotiations President Truman gave direct
aid to the shipowners by telling the press that he would
break the strike by the use of the Army, Navy, and the
War Shipping Administration. The President already
had broken the railroad strike by threats against the
Brotherhood of Railway Trainmen and Railroad Engineers.

The President had miscalculated on the degree of
unity that had been generated by the minimum demands
of CMU. Attempts to recruit scabs by government agencies fell flat. The President learned soon enough that the
ships would not move. To the solidarity of the CIO and
the AFL was added the publicly proclaimed support of
European maritime unions.

ISU President Harry Lundeberg, who on April 5 declared that "this is a very bad time in maritime industry
to go on strike" changed his strategy by June 15. Lundberg felt the pressure from his rank and file. *All* maritime
workers felt the June negotiations were to benefit the
entire industry. The victory of the CMU was the victory of each and every maritime worker on each and
every ship.

OPERATORS TRY TO FOSTER DISUNITY

But the shipowners had still another trick up their
sleeves. Less than two weeks after· the shipowners on the
East Coast had signed with the CMU, the West Coast
and Gulf operators granted wage increases to the Sailors'

Union of the Pacific which were $5 above those granted to the CMU. They granted increases to the SIU which were $10 above those of the CMU. This created an inequality which necessitated another strike in September to straighten out.

Again, upon the expiration of the ILWU contracts, September 30, 1946, the operators forced another showdown in the hope of forestalling maritime unity. During the strike, however, the ranks of the CMU held firm.

In the summer and fall of 1946, gains made by the licensed and unlicensed seamen were due only to the unity between *all* the maritime workers, AFL and CIO. This unity was not supported by Joseph P. Ryan and Harry Lundeberg, but was achieved in spite of them. The united thinking of the CMU discredited the attacks of Lundeberg and Ryan that the strikes were for "political" reasons.

The strikes in the summer and fall of 1946 netted the seamen considerable immediate gain. All of the demands presented were not granted upon the termination of the strike. The unresolved collateral issues were to be decided by an arbitrator.

The most outstanding gain that resulted from the struggle was the granting of the 48 hour week at sea and the 40 hour week in port besides a wage increase of $17.50 per month.

The arbitrator, whose award resulted in the termination of the September strike, ordered the payment of equal money for equal work. This decision went the furthest in the direction of eliminating differentials in wages and working conditions between different shipping companies.

In spite of the real gains made during the life of CMU,

it ˄was dissolved in the winter of 1947. Anticipating struggles in June, 1947, the CIO Maritime Committee met in San Francisco in May of 1947.

With the convening of the 80th Congress in January of 1947, the torrent of anti-labor legislation began.

The Taft-Hartley Bill was vetoed by President Truman on June 20. Both AFL and CIO in their campaign against the bill had characterized it as a slave bill. It was pointed out that the closed shop was prohibited, union security was abolished; it prevented bonafide collective bargaining, interfered with the right to strike, and, finally, all collective bargaining would be fettered and ultimately broken down by protracted proceedings in the courts. The labor injunction was revived, setting the clock back almost a half century. Under the guise of permitting suits against labor organizations, employers are given a free hand to raid union treasuries. A national union may be harassed by law suits which can be brought against them in any part of the country where they may maintain a local union. These law suits could be brought not only for alleged violations of contracts, but even for any damages resulting to the employer from a perfectly peaceful and otherwise lawful strike, resulting from the refusal of employees to work on scab products manufactured under substandard conditions.

President Truman, in his veto message, made the following prophetic observations:

When one penetrates the complex interwoven provisions of this omnibus bill, and understands the real meaning of its various parts, the result is startling.

The bill taken as a whole would reverse the basic direction of our national labor policy, inject the government into private economic affairs on an unprecedented scale, and conflict with important principles of our democratic society. Its provisions would cause more strikes, not fewer. It would contribute neither to industrial peace nor to economic stability and progress. It would be a dangerous stride in the direction of a totally managed economy. It contains seeds of discord which would plague this nation for years to come.

Congress overrode President Truman's veto, and the Taft-Hartley Bill became law June 23, 1947.

SHIPOWNERS ATTEMPT LOCKOUT

While the Taft-Hartley Bill was still being debated, the marine unions began to prepare for possible strike action if, on June 15, 1947, the shipowners refused to meet their demands. The West Coast longshoremen, the Marine Cooks & Stewards Union and the Marine Firemen, Oilers and Watertenders Union demanded that their contracts be renewed without making demands for improvements in these contracts.

To prepare for possible strike action at the expiration date of the 1947 contracts, the members of the CIO Maritime Committee met in San Francisco on May 15, 1947. It will be recalled that with the dissolution of the CMU, the CIO Maritime Committee undertook to act in behalf of all interested unions in the presentation of demands to their employers.

In so far as the West Coast unions merely demanded a renewal of their contracts, the NMU agreed to support these unions should a lockout be effected on the West Coast. On the East Coast the NMU was making demands for improvements in the contract then expiring. The NMU, in so far as it was making demands for the betterment of its contract, agreed not to demand strike support from the West Coast unions.

The National Maritime Union and the American Communications Association on the East Coast, notwithstanding the decision of the West Coast unions, presented a series of demands. Among the NMU demands were (1) wages and overtime increases; (2) the forty-hour week; (3) manning scales; (4) extension of vacations; (5) all ratings to be shipped through the union hall, and (6) health and welfare benefits.

On the deadline, on June 15, the shipowners on the East Coast had rejected all of the six demands. The unions then issued a notice to their membership that this attitude on the part of the shipowners constituted a lockout, and were advised that if the membership, through secret ballot to be counted on June 22, supported the strike, they would be directed to leave their ships. For three days all NMU crews on board vessels stood by. At 3 *A.M.* on June 19 the shipowners made an offer of a 5 per cent overall wage increase and payment for holidays, when they fall at sea. The seamen accepted this offer and the contract was renewed for another year.

It is difficult at this moment to determine the effectiveness of this limited kind of unity had a bitter struggle ensued. During the coming year, much deep study must be given to the establishment of organic unity in the maritime industry.

While in June 1947 shipowners could not move their ships because of an insufficient supply of labor, their profits were still enormous. They had almost no competition from foreign operators. In June of 1948 maritime workers may be faced with an entirely different situation. When the time comes, only organic unity will be adequate to meet the attack of the shipowners.

By the end of 1948 the shipowners, as all other employers, will have learned how to wield the weapon of the Taft-Hartley Bill, and if the maritime unions are not to be smashed, they must unite.

CIO radio operators—yes, even CIO licensed engineers —should join the unlicensed personnel in the organization of an industrial union of maritime workers.

Shipping is still good in 1947 and, as has already been indicated, will very likely continue to be good throughout 1947 and 1948; but that further inroads into the economic gains made by the seamen during the past decade will take place, there can be no doubt.

Fifty per cent of the workers now in the industry very likely participated in the struggles of 1934 to 1937. There may, perhaps, be a few still alive and active who can remember the 1921 struggles. But the 50 per cent who came into the industry during the war should heed the lessons of the past. To them, labor spies and the unconscionable attitudes of their employers are things they only read about.

There has already been much talk of a depression that may descend upon our land. Mean and ugly days may be in store for all workers. Merchant seamen, because their organizations are comparatively young, may suffer most. To the extent that experience fortified one for battle, the chronicle of events set out in this book should, it is hoped, in some small measure increase the chances for victory.

APPENDIX

1. That we terminate the strike and prosecute our demands for recognition of our duly elected representatives and for concluding union agreements with improved wages and working conditions with the NLRB.

2. That our duly elected officials stand instructed and authorized to represent us on all questions, concerning union agreements, wages and hours and working conditions.

3. That no final action shall be taken on this resolution until it has been discussed and acted upon by all ports at special meetings to be called immediately for this purpose.

4. In the event that all ports shall vote to concur in the above recommendations, no final action shall be taken until we have received assurances from the West Coast Joint Policy Committee that such action would not jeopardize the possibilities of our Brother Unions reaching a settlement on the West Coast.

5. And be it further resolved, that if our strike is concluded on the above basis and the shipowners still refuse to cooperate in trying to reach a settlement on all disputed issues, then the elected officials of our unions shall immediately call meetings in all ports to discuss what action shall be taken.

6. And be it further resolved, that if following conclusion of the strike here, the West Coast shipowners should attempt to block the settlement that now seems possible there, and if because of this the West Coast Unions should again ask for our support, our officials shall stand instructed to immediately take all steps possible to comply with their request.

7. And be it further resolved, that the strike is not to be terminated under any circumstances on the inter-coastal ships until such time as a complete and final settlement is arrived at with the West Coast Unions.

8. And be it finally resolved, that all ports be immediately notified by telegram of these recommendations and that they in turn notify the New York Strike Committee not later than Sunday afternoon at 5 P.M. of their decisions on our recommendations, and that these decisions be reported to the membership at a mass meeting, Sunday Evening, January 24.

BIBLIOGRAPHY

The following bibliography includes sources consulted. Direct reference by way of notes to the sources has been omitted. Original manuscripts indicate specific reference to the source material.

BOOKS

Abbot, Willis J. *American Merchant Ships and Sailors,* Dodd, Mead & Co., New York, 1902

Albrecht, Arthur Emil *International Seamen's Union of America,* Government Printing Office, Washington, D. C., 1923

Annin, Robert E. *Ocean Shipping,* Century Co., New York, 1920

Bimba, Anthony *History of the American Working Class,* International Publishers, New York, 1936

Brissenden, Paul *The I.W.W.: A Study of American Syndicalism,* Columbia University, New York, 1919

Calvin, H. C. and Stuart E. J. *The Merchant Shipping Industry,* John Wiley & Sons, New York, 1925

Foner, Philip S. *History of the Labor Movement in the United States,* International Publishers, New York, 1947

Foster, William Z. *From Bryan to Stalin,* International Publishers, New York, 1937

Healey, James C. *Foc's'le and Gloryhole,* Oxford University Press, New York, 1936

Hogle, Katherine *Maritime and General Strike of 1934,* Columbia University, New York, 1938, unpublished

Hudson, Roy *Four Fighting Years,* Marine Workers Industrial Union, New York, 1934 (pamphlet)

Hurley, Edward N. *The New Merchant Marine,* Century Company, New York, 1920

Hutt, Allen *The Post-War History of the British Working Class,* Coward McCann, New York, 1938

Lorwin, Lewis L. *Labor and Internationalism,* Macmillan Co., New York, 1929

Marvin, Winthrop *The American Merchant Marine,* Charles Scribner's Sons, New York, 1902

McMasters, James B. *History of the People of the United States,* D. Appleton and Co., 1905

Meany, George *American Federationist,* American Federation of Labor, November, 1940

Myers, Gustavus *History of the Great American Fortunes,* Random House, New York, 1936

New York City W.P.A. Writers' Project *Maritime History of New York,* Doubleday Doran, New York, 1941

Rippy, James Fred *Rivalry of the United States and Great Britain Over Latin America*, Johns Hopkins Press, 1929

Roosevelt, Franklin D. *Published Papers and Addresses*, Vol. I, Random House, New York, 1938

Swanstrom, Edward E. *The Waterfront Labor Problem*, Fordham University Press, New York, 1938

Taylor, Paul S. *Sailors Union of the Pacific*, Ronald Press, New York, 1923

Transport Workers International Propaganda and Action Committee, *Bevin and Wilson*, London, 1930 (pamphlet)

Wintringham, T. H. *Mutiny Through the Ages*, Fortuny's, New York, 1940

Zeis, Paul M. *American Shipping Policy*, Princeton University Press, 1938

Ziskind, David *One Thousand Strikes of Government Employees*, Columbia University Press, New York, 1940

GOVERNMENT PUBLICATIONS

Addresses by Senator LaFollette, *Congressional Record*, July 25 and August 1, 1921

Annual Reports submitted by the United States Maritime Commission for the years 1937, 1938, 1939, 1940, 1941 and 1942

Congressional Record, March 30, 1943, page 2755

Investigation of Air Mail and Ocean Mail Contracts, submitted by Senator Black, Report No. 898, 74th Cong. 1st Session, May, 1935

Post-War Outlook for American Shipping, report of the Post-War Planning Committee, June 15, 1946, United States Government Printing Office, Washington, D. C.

Use and Disposition of Ships and Shipyards at the End of World War II, report of the Harvard University Graduate School of Business Administration, Government Printing Office, Washington, D. C.

PERIODICALS AND PUBLICATIONS

American Communications Association, report of the International Executive Board, fifth annual convention, April 8-13, 1940, Chicago, Illinois

R. J. Baker *The American Merchant Marine*, Annals of the American Academy of Political Science, January, 1934

Convention proceedings of the International Seamen's Union of America, held in Washington, February, 1937

N.M.U. Convention proceedings, first, second, third, fourth and fifth conventions, held in 1937, New York; 1939, New Orleans; 1941, Cleveland; 1943, New York; and 1945, New York

NEWSPAPERS

The I.S.U. *Pilot* published between 1935 and 1937

The N.M.U. *Pilot* published between 1937 and 1947

COURT DECISIONS

Robertson v. Baldwin (SS Arago) 17 Sup. Ct. Reporter 331

Southern Steamship Co. v. N.L.R.B., 120 Fed. (2) 510

INDEX

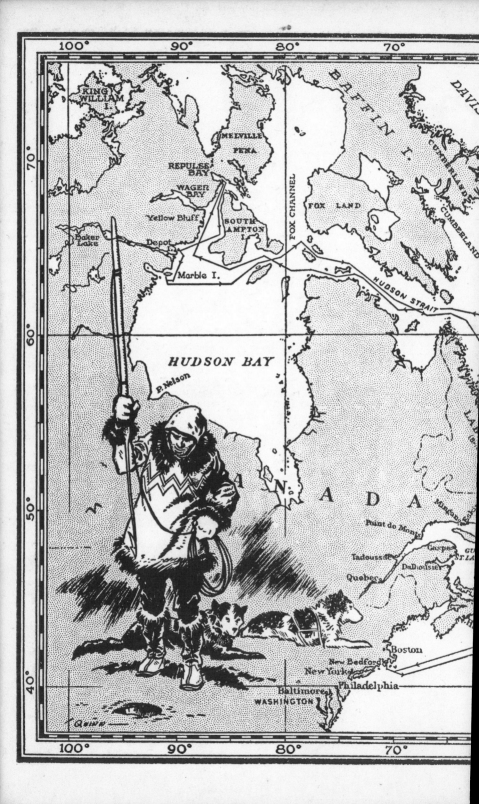